Corporate Citizenship and Sustainability: Measuring Intangible, Fiscal, and Ethical Assets

Corporate Citizenship and Sustainability: Measuring Intangible, Fiscal, and Ethical Assets

Jayaraman Rajah Iyer

Corporate Citizenship and Sustainability: Measuring Intangible, Fiscal, and Ethical Assets
Copyright © Business Expert Press, LLC, 2020.

All rights reserved. No part of this publication may be reproduced, stored in a retrieval system, or transmitted in any form or by any means—electronic, mechanical, photocopy, recording, or any other except for brief quotations, not to exceed 250 words, without the prior permission of the publisher.

First published in 2020 by
Business Expert Press, LLC
222 East 46th Street, New York, NY 10017
www.businessexpertpress.com

ISBN-13: 978-1-95253-816-2 (paperback)
ISBN-13: 978-1-95253-817-9 (e-book)

Business Expert Press Business Ethics and Corporate Citizenship Collection

Collection ISSN: 2333-8806 (print)
Collection ISSN: 2333-8814 (electronic)

Cover and interior design by S4Carlisle Publishing Services Private Ltd., Chennai, India

First edition: 2020

10 9 8 7 6 5 4 3 2 1

Printed in the United States of America.

Dedication

To my grandkids: Anoushka, Dhruv, and Mihika
The emerging Reverse Mentors

Abstract

Intangible is defined, like zero being found as a number. Intangible is proved as a constant, an energy force, with a fixed value in a specified mathematical context, enabling the accomplishment of an infinite succession of finite purposes by controlling each goal. Return on intangible inverts the corporate structure to create an equitable new stable element for corporate management, like that of the well-established mathematical and natural sciences. It enables preparing a CREAM—corporate governance, risk management, earnings, accounting quality, and management quality—Report measuring fiscal and ethical assets.

Furthermore, a blueprint for Gujarat state domestic product (GSDP) 2024 of $1.5 trillion, as illustrated in this book, establishes efforts per person (EPP) as the core denominator for development and plays a significant role in the construction of a macroeconomic model. Gross domestic product (GDP) figures are always delayed. The collateral damage, the delayed GDP data has inflicted on the UN Sustainable Development on Gross National Happiness (GNH) Index is obvious as the GNH index could not be linked to development. This has been rectified by bringing out a GDP–GNH combined index, covering the five criteria set by the CREAM Report. The bottom-to-top approach of preparing a CREAM Report and then providing a slot in the Creamchain for each individual enables participation and tracking the well-being and development for each person, individually and collectively at the same time.

Corporate citizenship is discussed. Since the days of Ashoka[1] in 300 BC, there is not a single century that could be termed as a civilizational era, anywhere in the world. It is so because social values have not been addressed at all. Corporate citizenship, therefore, is at the cusp of the modern-cum-corporate civilization, where a GDP–GNH connect can get an entry, the book argues.

---

[1] Ashoka the Great was an Indian emperor who ruled almost all of the Indian subcontinent from c. 268 to 232 BCE. Ashoka's edicts, in pillars and boulders and cave walls, distributed throughout the subcontinent brought out what might be called state, private, and individual morality. Author and historian H.G. Wells said, "Amidst the tens of thousands of names of monarchs that crowd the columns of history ... the name of Ashoka shines, and shines almost alone, a star." The Edicts of Ashoka, Ven. S. Dhammika: https://www.cs.colostate.edu/~malaiya/ashoka.html.

Keywords

action process; Action Value Capital; corporate citizenship; CREAM Report - corporate governance, risk management, earnings, accounting quality, management quality; CREAM Report framework: corporate social responsibility, corporate fiscal responsibility, corporate ethical responsibility, subject - object distinction of qualitative and quantitative elements of management; creative process; EPP: efforts per person; ethical assets; GNH Index: gross national happiness index; GRACE: governance, responsibility, authority, credibility, enablement; IBCM - Inactivity Based Cost Management; Intangible Value Capital; Intellectual Value Capital; RoI - Return on Intangible; Reverse Mentoring; Self-governance; Sustainability: sustainability of efficiency, sustainability of profits, sustainability of value system.

Table of Content

Preface .... *xi*
Acknowledgments .... *xvii*

Chapter 1   Causality 1
Chapter 2   Who Are YOU? 19
Chapter 3   Intangible Assets 41
Chapter 4   Intangible Defined 55
Chapter 5   Measuring the Intangible 67
Chapter 6   Inactivity Based Cost Management 81
Chapter 7   The Board of Directors the Corporate Proton ... 99
Chapter 8   The CEO Practices and CREAM Report for
             Corporate Electron 109
Chapter 9   Society for Corporate Neutron 121

About the Author *139*
Index *141*

Preface

Many observations and perspectives accumulated through my professional accounting experience have served as the inspiration for this book. The first came from an internship I worked at in 1966 when I joined Hindustan Lever Ltd. (HLL) under R. Subrahmanyan, then commercial services manager. A brilliant man, a chartered and cost accountant, he was working on product cost accounting. That was the year when the Government of India (GoI) had introduced cost audit for essential commodities, including one of HLL's major productions, *vanaspati*, a hydrogenated vegetable oil called Dalda. Every fortnightly Thursday, HLL would announce the price increase on the current cost of Dalda. The company factory at Sewri, Mumbai, would suspend dispatch until the price increase was cleared by the GoI, New Delhi. Dalda was so popular that millions of tin boxes of it were sold. Subh, as we called our boss, would continuously work on the product cost, adding every known allocated cost. At the time, there was a forward exchange market prevalent for vegetable oil. Subh would conscientiously work out the stock profit or stock loss for the commodity and make necessary adjustments for his cost submission to GoI. For a tin priced at Rs.25 (about $0.35 at today's $ rate), the price increase could have been a figure of 25 paise (1 percent). Cost audit from GoI was introduced later to several commodities, particularly pharma drugs. As I write this today, in 2019, the Indian prime minister Narendra Modi has introduced a scheme of providing quality medicines at affordable prices to the masses, called Jan-Aushadi Yojana, which supplies medicines at hardly 25 percent of the cost of branded drugs. A cost audit from the GoI put a stop to the exorbitant pricing policies of pharma companies. However, in 1983, when Dr Kaplan came up with activity based costing (ABC) it was a satisfying moment for Subh, who had taken note of several more cost drivers as early as 1966.

In 1992 when Dr Kaplan came up with the balanced scorecard (BSC), it influenced many minds and I was no exception. Linking the best of both ABC and BSC, I coined the term "inactivity based cost management."

In 1995, when the Internet was introduced in India via Videsh Sanchar Nigam Limited (VSNL), then the country's only telecommunication network, I got a telephone call from VSNL congratulating me for being the first registered user of India and was allocated the number BOMAAA001. I took the offer of the free webpage VSNL offered me and posted a one-page article on inactivity based cost management (IBCM). I recall seeing a book on ABC in the cabin of Mani Bharadwaj of PricewaterhouseCoopers (PwC) and discussed with him how IBCM could be of better use in management.

Later, in 2005, when called upon to do an RoI (return on investment) analysis for a huge investment in an ERP (enterprise resource planning) package by Mahindra British Telecom (MBT), I found it would be an exercise in futility, as there would be no cost savings as such for the investment. However, I said to the consulting firm that I could do a return on intangible for the same investment as to how the ERP package could be better utilized looking at its potential usage. Combining BSC, control objectives for information and related technology (COBIT) IT processes published by the Information Systems Audit and Control Association (ISACA)—an international professional association that focuses on IT governance—and IBCM, I gave detailed pre- and post-analytics for four issue areas: finance, project, human resources, and senior management. John Hugh, the CEO of MBT at that time, was quite impressed. The basis of IBCM is "Activity has a cost incidence whereas inactivity a cost consequence." As a policy, corporates should measure the cost consequence every day, tracking decisions already taken. Measuring inactivity for a machinery is easy whereas inactive elements in a person are difficult to measure. Return on intangible came to the rescue. I saw the potential of IBCM and promptly copyrighted the process with the Copyrights Office, GoI. IBCM with return on intangible gave a good foundation for corporate analytics for several issue areas as brought out by COBIT.

Working on wood accounting while I was a forestry operations accountant of WIMCO (a subsidiary of Swedish Match Company) in Mysore, in the south of India, also served up an interesting perspective. The Mysore branch supplied wood to two WIMCO factories—one in Ambernath (near Mumbai) and another at Chennai (in Tamil Nadu).

The accounting year for WIMCO was January to December whereas forestry operations took place between September and April, on the basis of the monsoon. So, at the beginning of an accounting year in January, factory costing would have to take note of wood felling from one season of the current season (September previous year to April current year) and 4 months from the next season (September to December current year, as part of next season September current year to April next year), which is unpredictable. It is unpredictable, as the foresters mark the trees for felling for the next season and start their work in the following September. I introduced a cost accounting method called the likely ultimate cost (LUC) for the factories to get a uniform cost throughout the year so that their monthly profitability statements would not fluctuate from month to month. LUC is the cost figure related to the end of the accounting year charges for the wood supplied but a standard cost from the beginning of the year. This LUC helped me in projecting a figure for the future and bringing it to today's level in the form of compound annual growth rate (CAGR) and compound annual reduction rate (CARR) converted into CDGR and CDRR (D-Daily), which you will see in this book.

I subsequently took up a consulting assignment for the Shipping Credit and Investment Company of India (SCICI) on cost accounting of shipping construction. SCICI was providing funds to shipowners at a low interest rate (a third of the prevailing bank rates). There were three parties to it: the shipowner, the shipbuilder, and SCICI. Shipowners taking the funds from SCICI would divert them to other than shipbuilding in their group companies. SCICI asked me to bring out shipping construction stages so that it could release funds according to the stages completed. This called for a detailed shipping construction manual, literally. While working on this, I found Japan's influence on the scenario in shipbuilding most interesting. After World War II, an air force veteran in Japan was entrusted with the charge of shipbuilding. He went around the globe visiting various shipyards and found they were building in the same pattern as before, from laying the keel upward. Being an air force man, he could not accept this practice and introduced the block development process of shipping construction. Different blocks constructed at the same time at different places and assembled at the shipyard reduced the time of construction substantially, from 16 years to 4 years. Placing an order 3 years in advance for items like the main engine, which would arrive in time for the requisite blocks, is an example of the kind of changes he effected. This book adopts the shipping process block technology for the preparation of a CREAM— corporate governance, risk management, earnings, accounting quality, and management quality—Report.

Martin Rees simplified physics to boost the understanding of how the universe works. When applied to corporates, not only does physics provide benchmarks and metrics but a simple two-process management. The application of these principles of physics leads to creating a basic management structure, which I call Corporate Atomic Structure in this book. I also include society in the structure. Corporate becomes a vibrant pulsating energy, making subatomic particles dance. Nobel laureate Murray Gellman described emergent property as that to which "you don't have to add anything more to get something more,"[1] something like a robust corporate yoga, fit as a fiddle. The holistic organizational structure, the Corporate Atomic Structure, created and quantified out of the practices listed in this book, will be complete in itself.

The last chapter is about society. I had the opportunity of working on a blueprint for Gujarat state domestic product (GSDP) 2024 of $1.5 trillion. It came in handy before the book went into the production line. GDP figures are brought out by departments of economics and statistics of governments in a leisurely manner. Then come the same delayed figures applied to the World Bank or the Organisation for Economic Co-operation and Development (OECD) and other international institutions. This must change. Furthermore, a blueprint for GSDP 2024 of $1.5 trillion, as illustrated in the book, establishes efforts per person (EPP) as the core denominator for development and plays a significant role in constructing a macroeconomic model. GDP figures are always delayed. The collateral damage, the delayed GDP data has inflicted on the UN Sustainable Development on Gross National Happiness (GNH)

---

[1] Quote from TED talk by M. Gell-Mann. 2007. "Beauty, Truth…. and Physics?" https://www.ted.com/talks/murray_gell_mann_beauty_truth_and_physics#t-872257.

Index, as suggested by the King of Bhutan, is obvious as the GNH index could not be linked to development. So much work on the field is done by many good NGOs, such as the Bill & Melinda Gates Foundation, that never gets measured. This is rectified by bringing out a GDP–GNH combined index, covering the five criteria set by the CREAM Report. The bottom-to-top approach of preparing a CREAM Report and then providing a slot in the Creamchain for each individual enables participation and tracking the well-being and development for each person, individually and collectively at the same time. EPP is significant because of the co-responsibility undertaken between governments and the people.

Then corporate citizenship is discussed. It is said Mahatma Gandhi made an observation when asked about what he thought of the Modern Civilization. He seems to have replied, that would be a good idea, giving the impression that modern civilization is yet to blossom.[2] His was a moral response to what he perceived as the evils of modern civilization. But it is a factual statement with or without a Gandhi in between. Since the days of Ashoka in 300 BC, there is not a single century that could be termed as a civilizational era, anywhere in the world. It is so because social values have not been addressed at all. For the first time, corporate social responsibility (CSR) has made an attempt and this book highlights the same into fiscal and ethical responsibility. By and large, corporate is in the same position as the East India Company was. Corporate citizenship, therefore, as part of the cusp of corporate civilization, with a GDP–GNH connect can get an entry, the book argues.

Jayaraman Rajah Iyer

---

[2]J.N. Sharma. "Hind Swaraj: A Fresh Look." https://www.mkgandhi.org/articles/hind_swaraj3.html.

Acknowledgments

It all started with Nigel Wyatt from London taking the trouble of recommending my name to the Publisher, Business Expert Press (BEP). Then thanks to Rob Zwettler and his team from BEP who have taken immense interest to get my work on for publishing. Great team to work with. I am indeed grateful to David Wasieleski, as incorporating his suggestions for improvement has given me a sense of satisfaction and a valid exposition of the concepts this book brings out. The teamwork was quite pronounced from Charlene Kronstedt and Sheri Dean, with Shyam Ramasubramony of S4Carlile Publishing Services perfecting the art of production line intricacies.

I want to thank my wife and children for their keen interest while I was writing this book. In particular, my daughter, Gayatri Jayaraman, who volunteered to check the book in all respects, editing, pinpointing errors, commenting "Not clear, unclear fragment, within two lines you have given three different names for the same organization, standardize subheads, qualifier? both what? check meaning—use better word etc. etc." I loved being the student.

The book *Eastern Religions and Western Thought* (1939) by Dr Radhakrishnan is truly an inspirational one with ethics, social values, and civilizations so beautifully expounded. I have been referring to it for several years, and the words of wisdom on ethics found in the book are so aptly applicable to the domain of modern-day corporate ethical responsibility.

Thanks guys!

CHAPTER 1

Causality

In our obscurity—in all this vastness—there is no hint that help will come from elsewhere to save us from ourselves. It is up to us.

—Carl Sagan*

Society's demands, in principle, are expectations arising out of ethical motives. When a joint-stock company is formed, by and large society welcomes such a business endeavor and participates willingly. The stock market is one of the points of investment for society and it is society's support for a corporate that churns out profits and ensures that dividends remain robust. Society becomes apprehensive when companies falter, and investments in mutual funds and pension funds fail to payback adequate returns, resulting in the loss of hard-earned income earned over several decades of employment. Society's expectation from a corporate is simple: Entrusting my money with you for safe keep. Period. Many companies do realize this factor and acknowledge that society sits at the top of all stakeholders. Corporate undertakes a fiduciary responsibility. A fiduciary is legally bound to act, within the confines of the law, in the best interests of the beneficiary. The beneficiary is society. Unfortunately, this responsibility is not always upheld. There are several cases of corporate negligence that abandon the fiduciary responsibility. When trust earned is lost, society's support is lost, and it is corporate that suffers ultimately. The corporate goes from being a joint-stock company to a deserted collection of individuals running from banker to banker. When an ethical motive is absent, profits dive. The key, which is what this book is about, is to highlight business enterprise motives toward the betterment of profits and growth while optimizing the trust factor.

---

*A Pale Blue Dot. https://www.planetary.org/explore/space-topics/earth/pale-blue-dot.html

Some recent major events in the realm of fiduciary responsibility are noteworthy. Volkswagen's diesel cheat software shook the world. It cost the company $33.6 billion,[1] the price for having allowed the cheat software through the front gate, duly authorized and signed by the board and the CEO. But a greater cost has been the loss of credibility for what had been one of the most trusted automotive brands in the world until the debacle. Hardly has the cost of dieselgate been counted, when Bayer's acquisition of Monsanto at $63 billion was followed by class-action lawsuits against Bayer in many countries. Glyphosate is being banned by countries like France and Germany. Roundup cancer lawsuits may cost Bayer tens of billions, says Top Class Actions.[2] The merger and acquisition of Autonomy resulted in Hewlett-Packard (HP) writing off $8.8 billion in Q4 of 2012. Toshiba's president and CEO, Hisao Tanaka, stepped down after an investigative panel found that company executives were complicit in misreported earnings. The incident highlighted "a systematic involvement including by top management."[3] Siemens's code of conduct was described by Joseph Murphy. as the "read, laughed and filed code."[4] To add to the agony is Carillion (2018),[5] which failed to "wake up and listen" to warnings. Two committees found that board minutes reveal a finance director was attempting to blow the whistle on accounting irregularities.

Tech giant Infosys and global conglomerate the Tata Group are said to have faltered on the corporate governance front, with respect to the conduct of Vishal Sikka, CEO of Infosys, and Cyrus Mistry, chairman of Tata Sons. The failure of infrastructure giant Infrastructure Leasing & Financial Services (IL&FS) has not only brought the entire Indian economy to a slowdown but has also highlighted the failure of individuals across the board. This collective pattern of failure represents a larger image of dreadful consequences. We are, however, at the cusp of corporate civilization, of do or die, make history or accept defeat.[6] Volkswagen, Bayer–Monsanto, Toshiba, HP–Autonomy, Carillion, and IL&FS are classic cases that define how a few at the helm can damage the entire future of industrial growth.

When we are looking at the corporate civilization, we are looking at the society we have formed. Society's constituents, if they remain in different layers, then corporate, which is part of the bigger canvas, will find somewhat irksome to be bracketed with all and sundry. Some may find it distasteful, if not irksome, when society finds the arrogant assumptions of inviolable authority, as displayed by Ferdinand Piëch, Volkswagen's chairman, before the scandal erupted. Piëch chided a lawyer for mispronouncing "Lamborghini." "Those who can't afford one, should say it properly," were his precise words.[7] A few people assume the right to decide on multibillion dollar commitments that impact society at large. Marc Benioff (2019), co-CEO of Salesforce and owner of *Time*, has pronounced that "capitalism, as we know it, is dead."[8] If so, the way corporate is run, from Lockheed to Enron to VW to Carillion to IL&FS, would ever be classified as capitalism. The society of different communities, which we do not know of fully, demands the answers. Marc Benioff (2019) calls for a new form of capitalism that focuses more on societal good. Societal good for one should be the same for another. Within the society's infrastructure, the new capitalism, as one part, should survive and endeavor to create a new corporate civilization.[9]

Corporate is missing the point. Their fault lines are visible, goalposts are missing, the future is bleak, and the present is shaky. Profits are the mainstay of corporate, and this is entrusted to and ensured by ethical motives. It is not a matter simply of a corporate giant bites the dust. There are 30 million micro, small and medium enterprises (MSME) in India. When a giant falls, the repercussions affect millions. The behavior of such failed business magnates further delays our collective commitments to the United Nations Millennium Declaration of sustainability of economic, social, environmental protection and development goals.

What has happened in India between 2004 and 2014 of the United Progressive Alliance (UPA) government is the aggrandizement of public wealth at the cost of extreme poverty. The consequences of the big corporate tree falling are now being made apparent. The Industrial Development Bank of India (IDBI), Industrial Credit and Investment Corporation of India (ICICI), and International Finance Corporation (IFC) as development institutions have disappeared, after writing off millions.[10] No one the wiser, but the agony is repeated. Lessons are not learned. Corporate must change, banking must change. Non-performing assets (NPAs) threaten the very basis of business survival. There's no connection between the declaration of sustainable goals and the tracking of such goals. Society remains in the iron age. For society, it's a signal to acknowledge the difficulty of essential survival.

Change, Change, Change Corporate! You are squandering away the riches of the earth. It is often said, "If you always do what you have always done, you will always get what you have always got." No longer can the promoter of a corporate entity afford to recklessly abandon the entity for society to bear the burden. This is what Benioff meant when he called upon America's top corporations to be responsible for improving society by serving all stakeholders ethically, morally, and fairly and not merely by boosting the stock price for shareholders.[11] In this work, we will examine what *ethically, morally, and fairly* means.

The late cosmologist Carl Sagan says we make our world significant by the courage of our questions and the depth of our answers. If society remains a passive observer, the degradation of industry is sure to follow. Paul Polman of Unilever urges, "Don't stay on the sidelines. It boils down to small actions, big difference. Together we can do it." He adds, "I don't like that word, responsibility. It is about co-responsibility." Till the emergence of corporate social responsibility (CSR), corporate could easily talk of business ethics, corporate governance, and so on without being attached to something called society. Corporate looks at itself as a giver of benefits and favor to the society, never to take responsibility for societal good. CSR has changed that. Paul Polman has done yeoman service to the society by his Sustainable Living Plan project through Unilever in the last decade. He would surely agree with the willingness of the society and the enthusiasm with which it has taken to his call for co-responsibility, however limited Unilever's interaction with it. Small actions do make a big difference, as he rightly observes. However, from the society, it is not co-responsibility but a sense of consequent responsibility that corporate must clearly understand. Bayer invests in Monsanto a $63 billion and comes a cropper. Society looks at companies that invest wisely and benefit society. Society has no means of advising the board as to what and how they function. It is the corporate that needs to go to the society regarding its intentions to execute a multibillion dollar investment. This work expands CSR to corporate fiscal responsibility (CFR) and corporate ethical responsibility (CER). CER of the corporate defines its ethical responsibility and then the consequent responsibility undertaken by the society is truly a quid pro quo.

Former secretary-general of the UN Kofi Annan while releasing the United Nations Convention Against Corruption (UNCAC) document said,

> Corruption is an insidious plague that has a wide range of corrosive effects on societies. It undermines democracy and the rule of law, leads to violations of human rights, distorts markets, erodes the quality of life and allows organized crime, terrorism and other threats to human security to flourish.[12]

UNCAC is one of the finest, rather the finest, document ever written, for two of its articles: (1) Article 13, Participation of Society, and (2) Article 10, Public Reporting. These statutes best exemplify Abraham Lincoln's words: A government of the people, by the people, for the people shall not perish from the earth. A corporate setup is created by the people. Article 13, Participation of Society, of the UNCAC ensures the dictum of the people, and Article 10, Public Reporting, endows the rights for the people to get the reports back. As President Barack Obama said during his inaugural address to Congress, "Here in Washington, we've all seen how quickly good intentions can turn into broken promises and wasteful spending." Society needs to get qualitative data, for sure. UNCAC Article 13 could have cautioned corporate before it implanted a cheat software. UNCAC Article 10 could have ensured the concept of co-responsibility was executed by the declaration of ethical assets.

The participation of a society is a matured extension of people electing a government. What society wants from corporate is a confirmation of an intrinsic value system. Article 10 of the UNCAC, Public Reporting, ensures the people know what their own roles are and what the government's role is. Society, at the top of the pyramid of stakeholders, has been demanding more and more transparency from corporate and is dissatisfied with the less and less it is being given. Despite government-enacted laws and active ingredients from regulatory bodies, corporate evades the core demands and is indeed found wanting. It remains aloof from happenings that demand corrections. It is stubborn in its isolation from society. There is no need for such a disconnect. All corporate has to do is to quantify and make known its ethical values. These two articles of the UNCAC would go a long way to satisfy the demands of society.

As a first step toward corporate governance, align fiscal responsibility with ethical responsibility. For example, before a drug can be prescribed in the United States it must undergo the Food and Drug Administration (FDA) approval process. Once approved, drug companies stand to benefit. This process is aligning fiscal responsibility with ethical responsibility that the FDA inspects to ensure compliance with the laws and good manufacturing practice (GMP). Similar management practices applied to each area of management are termed as corporate governance. Aligning all issue areas in a company would be critical to an overall assessment of corporate governance, without an exception. This includes a code of conduct or code of business principles (CoBP) or Whistleblower Policy or UNCAC or United Nations Global Compact (UNGC) covering 10 principles that are meant to benefit a company and typify the value system practiced. These have to be adopted by a company in detail for governance of each such issue area. That document so prepared is a tangible substance of quality, as good as installed machinery. Such documents, which are very many mandatory as well as nonmandatory policy documents, fall under the head *management quality*. This is a repository of policy statements a company adheres to. When effectively practiced, the result would be the measurement of corporate governance. Just as detailed factory inspections and audits to check and certify GMP or total quality management (TQM) practices are verified, corporate governance certification is to be verified. When an issue area is present in management quality that becomes the Cause. When measured and certified for compliance with such a policy, the Effect is assessed. The balance of these is corporate governance. Just as a six sigma process is established for manufacturing, a similar six sigma process improvement for corporate governance is established. Management quality and corporate governance would go hand in hand as effectively and surely as Newton's Third Law of Motion: For every action, there is an equal and opposite reaction. Establish management quality to precede corporate governance. The cheat software got in because the company skipped the deference to management quality.

Volkswagen was awarded the Best Corporate Governance for the Automotive Sector for 2014 in Europe by *Ethical Boardroom*. It was reminiscent of the AAA ratings that Standard & Poor's (S&P), Moody's, and Fitch granted companies like Bear Stearns, Fannie Mae, Freddie Mac, and Lehman Brothers before they collapsed. IL&FS credit ratings were equally misstated. In the case of Volkswagen, there was no policy document to show that a cheat software would be against their CoBP policies, although Volkswagen had prepared a detailed code of conduct for the group. This document lists several international conventions followed, such as the International Covenant on Economic, Social and Cultural Rights (1966), in addition to the laws and regulations for the countries.

After the deluge, society is not aware whether any adequate measures have now been taken that were missing earlier in CoBP. When there's no such correction made, fiscal responsibility doesn't align with ethical responsibility. There are also cases where clear written policies exist but are cast aside under the "read, laughed and filed code." This will be the case in general for all companies where the effort is not made to align fiscal and ethical responsibilities. One will see a long list of policy statements under management quality with no corresponding compliance under corporate governance. However, when such an event like the Volkswagen case explodes, the general reaction is lack of corporate governance, which is questioned immediately. In this context, a corresponding perspective comes from Hermes EOS, the stewardship division of Hermes Investment Management, one of the major stakeholders in Volkswagen, which called for an overhaul of the management and corporate governance culture at Volkswagen. There was no such corporate governance culture, Volkswagen displayed. Aligning fiscal responsibility with ethical responsibility is going to be paramount for companies to be just and equitable.

What Paul Polman said in 2010 are the same value statements made by Marc Benioff today but remain as relevant for companies that seek to be just and equitable. Business ethics has indeed become just lip service. Companies would not even file a balance sheet if it was not mandatory. Corporates will remain required to communicate voluntarily just and equitable practices to society by Article 10 of the UNCAC, until it becomes mandatory, which it will only when society insists.

Mandatory regulations are imposed by a government but at the insistence of society. Society is not a nonentity; it is a powerful apparatus when the government listens.

There are three distinct pronounced areas for corporate to note:

1. Management quality, which is a repository of policies.
2. Corporate governance, which involves the practices of the CEO team.
3. Society or people, who usher in changes inside corporate through the government and regulatory bodies.

These three Ps of management—policy, practices, and people—are the crux of management of corporate affairs that we shall discuss in the coming chapters. There are clear boundaries and functions for each, a clear-cut set of duties to perform, a responsibility to participate, and accountability to own.

Business enterprise is a profound thought of good intentions toward society that sets apart corporate culture over individual choice. A culture is a function of true knowledge of awareness, an identity with ethical responsibility, that by which corporate infers and society teaches. The ethical motive, incorporated at the time of registration for a joint-stock company, remains untouched. "Just and equitable" is not an expression of political statement for voters, but an invitation for stakeholders to vote with their wallet. Money is business, to attract money in business, state your stand. Measure it so that society understands it as a testimony of your will and actions. Just and equitable should have a reference to the context, and so should "societal good," instead of being merely a catchword, for catchwords face the issue of being unexamined and unanalyzed over a while. They just disappear for another new catchword. Society remains confused and disordered. Practically, the society does not respond, and the catchwords remain the monopoly of a few.

Bring data to society's table. Writing to the board of Infosys during the previous Vishal Sikka imbroglio, the Infoscions, an organization of former employees, said, "In God we trust; everyone else brings data to the table used to be our adage in everything we did and there were no exceptions!" This is a good adage that can be extended to society and shall be served a measured qualitative data at the table without exception. First of all, let corporate create a platform for qualitative data within whereas this book recommends bringing the data to society's table. Here we are looking at qualitative data, such as the code of good conduct. Disclosure of such data is going to improve upon a company's reputation. If you are doing well, do not withhold such data. If you are practicing and measuring the code of conduct of every employee in your company and your grade reveals that you are excelling, make it known to the society. The dignity and responsibility of an individual are recognized, a sense of honor. Contrarily, very many companies in India are marching toward insolvency procedures, all at the same time, because of the Modi government introducing the Insolvency and Bankruptcy Code (IBC). This has ended crony capitalism. The slate is clean for doing good business in India, for those who are ready to go for a corruption-free business model.[13] NPAs would surely be a thing of the past. Corporate governance is the governance standard for the value system within a company. Measuring quantitative data is already in existence, nothing more to be added to it. Value system is existing for a few but not measured. By measuring the value system, corporate governance makes itself known.

Let us move forward in our endeavor to establish qualitative data that is measurable, meaningful first of all within corporate, and then communicable to society. Note, society already recognizes how corporate uses ethical assets, and ethical performance establishes how just and equitable corporates are discharging their fiduciary duties, not merely fiscal assets, which are the domain of market speculators. Toshiba, Enron, Worldcom, and many more tampered with their balance sheets and failed miserably. Fiscal assets have a limited period usage, of use and throw. Ethical assets are the mainstay of your organization. Bring a list of ethical assets to society's table. They are intangible. In the sense ethical assets are everlasting, they would remain the backbone of an organization. Intangible as everlasting is one thing but remaining the backbone of the organization is another. The former is a time factor but the latter warrants positioning.

Dr Radhakrishnan (Indian philosopher and former president of India) mentions Pascal's well-known classification of the ways to belief, custom, reason, and inspiration suggests three stages of mental evolution—sense, reason, and intuition—though they are not to be regarded as chronologically successive and separate. In youth, we rise from the empirical to the dialectical stage when we argue and derive conclusions from observed data. At a more mature stage, we obtain a synthetic and intuitive knowledge of reality by means of an experience that embraces the whole soul. But intuition, though it includes the testimony of will and feeling, is never fully attained without strenuous intellectual effort. It cannot dispense with the discipline of reason and the technique of proof. He goes on to warn that the intuitive consciousness is not to be confused with the instinctive.[14]

Instinctive is a term we associate with reaction and intuitive with knowledge, from gross to subtle. The dictionary meaning of it, however, describes instinctive as one without conscious thought and intuitive as one without conscious reasoning, and as the expression goes many a slip between the cup and the lip. When we analyze the three stages of mental evolution, senses are related to instinctive reaction, reason to logical knowledge, which Dr Radhakrishnan says is comparable to a finger that points to the object and disappears when the object is seen, whereas intuitive knowledge is to a higher wavelength of the discipline of reason with the technique of proof. All three have a common thread: Instinctive reaction relates to a physical effort, reasoning to an intellectual effort (to trigger the finger to go in search of an object or a solution), and intuitive knowledge to an intellectual effort of egoistic discrimination. It's personal, the domain where a single dot produces several patents by different people, each unique. The one that is common to all, as the gems strung together that may vary in color and species, but the supporting string is the same all through, is intangible. Intangible is an effort, an energy force to be reckoned with. Intangible is all pervasive. Intangible influences actions and identifies inactions simultaneously, when energy force is absent, that is, without conscious thought or conscious reasoning. Intangible is a constant, enabling to derive a fixed value in a specified mathematical context, for example, return on intangible.

Illustratively, in an age-old country-music album, the song "Deck of Cards" by Tex Ritter goes like this:

A boy soldier being caught with playing cards in church, was brought before Provost Marshall. After warning of dire consequences, the soldier did narrate an interesting story. Sir, after marching for six days neither I had a Bible nor a Prayer Book that I spread the deck of cards I had, in the church. You see sir, when I look at the Ace it reminds me that there is but one God. Two, Old and the New Testament. Three, Father, Son and the Holy Ghost. He goes on. The King, the Queen, the jack or knave. Sir, I count the number of spots in a deck I find three-hundred-sixty-five—the number of days in a year, Fifty-two cards—the number of weeks in a year, Twelve picture cards—number of months, thirteen tricks—the number of weeks in a Quarter. Four colors—the number of seasons in a year. Sir, my pack of cards serves me as a Bible, an almanac and a prayer book.

Provost Marshall who warned of the dire consequences was left wondering how the boy soldier could count the fiscal assets—the deck of cards—solve a puzzle, and also retain the ethical assets. Connecting the different perspectives, the human mind focuses on the behavior of highly sensitive dynamical systems, given access to a constant.

Understanding the Intangible—A CERN Perspective

Let us peep into the minds of the scientists of the European Organization for Nuclear Research, known as CERN, a little bit. On June 18, 2004, an unusual new landmark was unveiled at CERN, a 2-meter high statue of the Indian deity Shiva Nataraja, the Lord of Dance. The statue, symbolizing Shiva's cosmic dance of creation and destruction, was given to CERN by the Indian government to celebrate the research center's long association with India. Shiva's cosmic dance then became a central metaphor in Austrian-born American physicist, systems theorist, and deep ecologist Fritjof Capra's international bestseller *The Tao of Physics*. A special plaque next to the Shiva statue at CERN explains the significance of the metaphor. Capra finds a similarity between modern physics and Shiva, not only in terms of the birth and death of living creatures, but also the very essence of inorganic matter. Shiva's dance is the dance of subatomic matter that, Capra says, "unifies ancient mythology, religious art, and modern physics" (Figure 1.1)[15]

12 CORPORATE CITIZENSHIP AND SUSTAINABILITY

Figure 1.1 The Shiva's cosmic dance statue at CERN
Photo Credit: Giovanni Chierico.

Plato's Cave

Writing about Shiva's statue, Aidan Randle-Conde, a postdoctoral student at CERN, looks at it from two different angles. During the daytime, Shiva reminds us that the universe is constantly shaking things up, is remaking itself, and is never static, she says, and by night, when we have more time to contemplate the deeper questions, Shiva literally casts a long shadow over our work, a bit like the shadows on Plato's cave.[16] This is an interesting observation that can be extended to the corporate model.

A comparative study of CERN and corporate throws some light on the existence of matter and its creation of energy. It is critical to the very existence of corporate, what it does, how it could use its capability for a sustainable, trouble-free future of industry and commerce. CERN states, (a) subatomic matter not only performs an energy dance, but also is an energy dance and (b) subatomic matter does not remain static. We shall restrict subatomic matter to protons, neutrons, and electrons for this work, which primarily establishes the connect between corporate and nature. Then we shall look into whether corporate is stuck in Plato's cave.

Lessons derived from CERN would bring metaphysics and physics into fusion. In other words, aligning fiscal responsibility with ethical responsibility. Corporate is masquerading under the claim of secrecy, unwilling to publish qualitative data that would be detrimental to their own progress vis-à-vis the competition. Measuring management quality, a repository of mandatory as well as nonmandatory rules and regulations adopted by a company, is necessary. So would be other qualitative data: accounting quality, risk management, and corporate governance. The reality is not that corporate doesn't want to release the data, but rather that corporate doesn't have any data to publish. In the aftermath of the Toshiba expose, news of manipulation of accounting emerges. In the aftermath of cheat software, Volkswagen is left defending multibillion dollar class-action lawsuits. Whistleblowers did their job, and energy giant Enron went through bankruptcy and saw the dissolution of Arthur Andersen, one of the Big 5 audit firms. In the aftermath of the London Inter-bank Offered Rate (LIBOR) being used to tamper with rates, the risk appetite in the top echelons of Barclays bank/group forces their chairman to resign. The inability of corporate to measure metaphysical concepts is more than clear. Even at the height of the BP Deepwater oil spill disaster in the Gulf of Mexico, the total expenditure was said to be about $2 billion. Not so long after HP entered into a merger and acquisition with Autonomy, a write-off of $8.8 billion became inevitable, which shows how ridiculous it is to be unaware of a company's qualitative performance at the time of acquisition. Such a failure does not reflect on HP alone but on the four major firms that negotiated the deal. These Big 4 audit firms continue their legacy of ineffectiveness in the Carillion fiasco too. That the next chief financial officer had to go through whistleblowing procedures to get her concerns about accounting irregularities taken seriously by the Carillion board is extraordinary, according to the report.[17] Now, Big 4 firms are being investigated by the Serious Fraud Investigation Office (SFIO), GoI, in the case of the fraud in IL&FS.[18] That's the last straw that broke the camel's back. One can legitimately say corporate management is utterly depraved and incapable of establishing a value system, crucial to establish the tenets of the righteousness of corporate civilization.

Corporate Is Living in Plato's Cave

In Plato's cave, the chained prisoners could only see the shadow on the front wall, not the action of puppeteers behind them. They have no concept of reality as they never look back but look only at what plays out on the front wall. One of the prisoners breaks free and runs outside to acquire knowledge. He returns to the cave to explain the reality to the remaining prisoners. They think he is stupid. They resist any attempt to free them. Corporate is living in Plato's cave. They are unwilling to see energy in its pure form. Companies are injured but the remedy is being rejected. The vision for ethical responsibility must evolve from within; it cannot be administered through external consulting. As Carl Sagan reminds us, there is no hint that help will come from elsewhere; corporate resides in a do-it-yourself domain.

Chapter 1: Causality: Points to Ponder

We know the cause, corporate intransigence, and the effect, lack of values.

1. Society's demands: Corporate lack of concern toward society despite hundreds of regulations being brought in is indeed quite telling. This will change when companies imbibe value systems within that would attract society to invest more in such companies.

2. Corporate is missing the point: The point is sustainability. Without a value system, companies cannot sustain for long. Benioff calling upon U.S. top corporations to be responsible for improving society by serving all stakeholders—ethically, morally, and fairly—is the point to be noted and change effected.
3. Adopt the UNCAC Template: Article 13, Participation of Society, and Article 10, Public Reporting, would go a long way to stabilize corporate initiatives toward the betterment of corporate profits and growth. These two articles are the links between corporate and society, establishing co-responsibility.
4. Aligning Fiscal Responsibility with Ethical Responsibility: Societal good means corporate ethical motive is a well-written plan of action. Currently, corporate is not looking at ethical motive as a principal mover of profits and growth. They are completely engrossed in attaining fiscal targets. Aligning the two would make the difference.
5. Bring the Data to Society's Table: This is Article 10, Public Reporting. A list of ethical assets of a company would reveal what data is relevant and would interest society. Note, society is the investor in your company.
6. Intangible—A CERN Perspective: –It opens up a perspective on antimatter the Large Hadron Collider (LHC) tries to decipher. This could also be an eye-opener for CERN to learn from, understanding and deriving intangible, to locate the missing antimatter.
7. A comparative study of CERN and Corporate: There are a lot of similarities between what CERN does and what corporate does, finding the meaning of matter and antimatter, physics and metaphysics, tangible and intangible, non-pulsating energy and pulsating energy, growth and profits.

Action Point

1. Corporate is living in Plato's cave. Opportunity to listen to the prisoner who had gone out and seen the world of energy should be taken.

Notes

1. G. Kable. 2019. "Volkswagen's Dieselgate Costs Top $33.6 Billion." https://www.wardsauto.com/industry/volkswagen-s-dieselgate-costs-top-336-billion.
2. S. Datko. 2019. "Roundup Cancer Lawsuits May Cost Bayer Tens of Billions," *Top Class Action*. https://topclassactions.com/lawsuit-settlements/consumer-products/roundup-cancer-lawsuits-may-cost-bayer-tens-of-billions.
3. R. Savage. 2015. "Toshiba's $1.2bn Accounting Scandal and the Problem with Japanese Corporate Governance." https://www.managementtoday.co.uk/toshibas-12bn-accounting-scandal-problem-japanese-corporate-governance/article/1356743.
4. OECD. "Mr. Joseph E. Murphy (Corporate Compliance and Ethics Professional)." In: *Review of the OECD Anti-Bribery Instruments: Compilation of Responses to Consultation Paper*, March 31, 2008. http://www.oecd.org/daf/anti-bribery/anti-briberyconvention/40773471.pdf.
5. Sky News. 2018. "Carillion Failed to 'Wake Up and Listen' to Warnings." https://news.sky.com/story/carillion-failed-to-wake-up-and-listen-to-warnings-11269033.
6. J. Iyer. 2015. "Who failed Infosys, Is It Corporate Governance or Management Quality?" https://www.linkedin.com/feed/update/urn:li:activity:6309431719099490304.
7. J. Useem. 2016. "What Was Volkswagen Thinking? On the Origins of Corporate Evil—and Idiocy." https://www.theatlantic.com/magazine/archive/2016/01/what-was-volkswagen-thinking/419127/.
8. P.R. La Monica. 2019. "Marc Benioff Says Capitalism, As We Know It, Is Dead." https://edition.cnn.com/2019/10/04/business/marc-benioff-capitalism-dead/index.html.
9. Ibid.
10. India Today. 2011. "Scandals during UPA Rule." https://www.indiatoday.in/india/photo/scandals-during-upa-rule-365055-2011-02-15/7.
11. P.R. La Monica. 2019. "Marc Benioff Says Capitalism, As We Know It, Is Dead." https://edition.cnn.com/2019/10/04/business/marc-benioff-capitalism-dead/index.html.
12. UN_Convention_Against_Corruption.pdf—United Nations Office on Drugs and Crime, Vienna.

13. Economic Times. 2019. "10,860 Cases under IBC Pending before NCLT at the End of September: Govt." https://economictimes.indiatimes.com/news/economy/policy/10860-cases-under-ibc-pending-before-nclt-at-the-end-of-september-govt/articleshow/72348493.cms?utm_source=contentofinterest&utm_medium=text&utm_campaign=cppst.
14. S. Radhakrishnan. 1939. *Eastern Religions and Western Thoughts* (London, UK: Oxford University Press), p. 113.
15. Fritj of Capra. 2004. "Shiva's Cosmic Dance at CERN." https://www.fritjofcapra.net/shivas-cosmic-dance-at-cern/.
16. A. Randle-Conde. 2011. "In the shadow of Shiva." https://www.quantumdiaries.org/2011/11/10/in-the-shadow-of-shiva/.
17. Sky News. "Carillion Failed."
18. S. Dave, S. Shukla. 2019. "Serious Fraud Investigation Office Lens on IL&FS Auditors." https://economictimes.indiatimes.com/industry/banking/finance/serious-fraud-investigation-office-lens-on-ilfs-auditors/articleshow/69658026.cms.

CHAPTER 2

Who Are YOU?

> *Animal spirits—a spontaneous urge to action rather than inaction, and not as the outcome of a weighted average of quantitative benefits multiplied by quantitative probabilities.*
>
> —John Maynard Keynes*

Individual unleashing of energy and getting credit for it is the new form of capitalism. In art, in literature, in music, in sports, individuals gain renown, not the corporate entity that promotes them, be it a sports club or an opera house. Marc Benioff's calls for a new form of capitalism are timely, as the hierarchical one-man call center model, a model where delegation of authority doesn't exist, no longer works. Paul Polman, citing Winston Churchill says, "However, just like democracy, the alternatives to capitalism have all been tried and all been found wanting—some, like communism, catastrophically so."[1] Just as Samuel Johnson said of marriage, that it may have its own pains, but celibacy has no virtue. Correspondingly, co-responsibility is the keyword for partnership between a joint-stock company and society. Flawed as it may be, there is no viable alternative to this partnership. Industry shall flourish once the pains of marriage are removed. There will be a change, the realignment of forces. Corporate has misused freedom of enterprise as a catchword and that needs thorough scrutiny. There are two distinct areas at the forefront: conflict of conscience and freedom of individuals.

We have been in search of a new capitalism for too long. Economic self-interest dominated centuries of trade and commerce. It is the same today, with the MAGA—Make America Great Again—campaign by

---

*ISN ETH Zurich The General Theory of Employment, Interest, and Money By John Maynard Keynes 1366_KeynesTheoryofEmployment.pdf p.81. https://www.files.ethz.ch/isn/125515/1366_KeynesTheoryofEmployment.pdf

President Trump. This is commonplace for all ages. However, if we are looking for a new capitalism, it is the ethics of capitalism that need an emphatic emphasis. The current practice of corporate leadership "is not about giving energy, but unleashing other's people energy," says Polman.[2] It is indeed the definition of capitalism—ownership of one's energy. Energy cannot be taken away. Corporate now needs to measure the unleashing of energy and ensure that those individuals that do, get due credit for it. With this, the freedom of individuals is activated in an organization, and with it, the embracing of accountability. Within corporate's own closed walls, responsibility resonates with co-responsibility. From the foot soldier level upward, individuals are ready to take on responsibility. Hitherto, co-responsibility has not been practiced within the corporate. It's only put on display as a facade, for the benefit of a watchful society. Polman's method of bringing data to society's table, in the way co-responsibility is practiced at Unilever, would be more useful for society to learn. Corporate ethical motive, ushered in within a company first, eliminates the need for whistleblowing. The way to do this is to remove the barrier between the highest paid and the lowest paid, and then measure ethical responsibility, as all stand equal. The conflict of conscience is removed. Then the experiment can be extended to society. Bring the abstractions into reality, acknowledge value where value is due, and deconstruct what is valueless. That is the new form of capitalism, ethically, morally, and fairly implemented.

Corporate history is replete with many misgivings, tolerating the idiosyncrasies of many a CEO. The sociologist Diane Vaughan says, "Normalization of deviance is a cultural drift in which circumstances classified as 'not okay' are slowly reclassified as 'okay'." Ushering in CER cannot be postponed. At this juncture let us briefly check on what John Maynard Keynes had to say about it. By defining Animal Spirits, Keynes takes us to that level of understanding of what corporate shall look into and learn. He says,

> Even apart from the instability due to speculation, there is the instability due to the characteristic of human nature that a large proportion of our positive activities depend on spontaneous optimism rather than mathematical expectations, whether moral or hedonistic or economic. Most, probably, of our decisions to do something positive, the full consequences of which will be drawn

out over many days to come, can only be taken as the result of animal spirits—a spontaneous urge to action rather than inaction, and not as the outcome of a weighted average of quantitative benefits multiplied by quantitative probabilities.

All that we list of corporate failures, Keynes captures precisely. Our disasters are man-made, and they are repeated. No company is geared to avert such disasters. If we recognize the instability of human nature, we should take steps on how to measure such human nature that leads to the instability of the corporate, the world over.

Moral, hedonistic, and economic classifications correspond with the good, bad, and ugly scenarios in relation to corporate sustainability.

Moral

Morality does not come of its own. We teach ethics in schools but propagate greed once the same students reach a business school. Conflict of interest, conflict of personal interest, and conflict of conscience have to be seen from a corporate perspective and need quantification. We can't leave them to the hands of God. We have to quantify within the corporate walls, the acts of people who disregard the very basis of morality that society has given birth to, after hundreds of years of justice and democratic principles. Defining moral, measuring ethics, identifying the behavior of employees, workers, or CEOs, we are looking for an environment for the growth of values. What we see within corporate is a representative sample of the society at large. We have people in MNCs traveling the globe and undertaking to conform to the rules and laws of the lands they visit. It is the fiduciary duty of corporate to create an environment of moral values. We cannot hesitate to ask and must get answers, should we look for a civilizational approach to corporate history. When moral rules are violated, social chaos is bound to raise its ugly head.

Hedonistic

Charles Ferguson's documentary film *Inside Job* notes the hedonism rampant in Wall Street. In it, Jonathan Alpert, a therapist whose clients include many high-level Wall Street clients, says,

These people are risk-takers, they are impulsive. And that manifests outside of work as well. It's quite typical for the guys to go out, to go to strip bars, to use drugs. I see a lot of cocaine use, a lot of use of prostitution. He goes on to add, there's just a blatant disregard for the impact that their actions might have on, on society, on family. They have no problem using a prostitute, uh, and going home to their wife.[3]

That's corporate hedonism in action for you.

Economic

The third instability Keynes mentions is economic. Look at the list from Lockheed in 1976, when Lockheed Aircraft Corp. admitted to a payoff of $24 million during a Senate subcommittee meeting. The revelations exposed the bribing of key world leaders—Prime Minister Tanaka of Japan, Prince Bernhard of Belgium, and Columbian and Italian top brass were among the major beneficiaries. Corruption continues despite the UNCAC, despite the Foreign Corrupt Practices Act (FCPA), despite the Sarbanes–Oxley Act (SOX), despite the Organisation for Economic Co-operation and Development (OECD) study on anti-bribery. The Augusta Westland VVIP chopper scam is rattling now in India, after the main culprits, Christian Michel and Ratul Puri, have been arrested by the Enforcement Directorate (ED), long after the Bofors scandal, in which Rajiv Gandhi, the then Prime Minister of India, was allegedly involved.[4,5] It never stops. An OECD study on anti-bribery instruments cites Joseph Murphy, a corporate compliance and ethics professional and a participant in the study. In it, Murphy says, "Governance is not compliance and ethics" and disputes the OECD's assumption that large multinational companies generally have adequate internal compliance controls.

> One need only look at the record at Siemens, whose code of conduct was described as the 'read, laughed and filed code,' or the long, legalistic (and ineffective) code that existed at Enron to see the great danger in such sweeping conclusions.[6]

Economic disasters are man-made, and we seem to have no current means of arresting them. Bad management of corporate affairs, costing a company heavily, with disastrous economic consequences, is blamed on the company. The perpetrators go free. This book is unique in the sense that there is no separate company rating but combined ratings based on the performance of individuals would constitute company ratings. Each person is rated and simultaneously his or her inactivity. An Index of Inactivity is prepared for each, which reflects the cost consequence of nonperformance daily. Shirking the shoulders and getting away is not possible.

Indian Companies Act 2013

In the Indian Companies Act 2013, under Code for Independent Directors, the first listed is, "An independent director shall uphold ethical standards of integrity and probity."[7] Never mind that there is no code of conduct for directors while independent directors are given one. There is no mention of how they are going to measure it, neither for the independent directors nor for the other directors of the board.

In the 2013 Committee of Sponsoring Organizations of the Treadway Commission (COSO) Framework and SOX Compliance, ethical values are listed as the primary concern under the 17 Principles of a Control Environment. The first "demonstrates commitment to integrity and ethical values." The COSO Framework defines the Control Environment in the following manner:

> The control environment sets the tone of an organization, influencing the control consciousness of its people. It is the foundation for all other components of internal control, providing discipline and structure. Control environment factors include the integrity, ethical values, and competence of the entity's people; management's philosophy and operating style; the way management assigns authority and responsibility and organizes and develops its people; and the attention and direction provided by the board of directors.[8]

In the Volkswagen emissions scandal, we are unaware of the persons who cleared planting the cheat software in millions of vehicles. The CEO and the board are two separate entities within an organization. The board is responsible for management quality, that is to say, discharging fiduciary duty that brings out rules of ethics, a set of policies, whereas corporate governance is domain of the CEO team. If there is no written policy toward not creating a cheat software, then the CEO is free to act as he did in Volkswagen. In China, there is a proverb, if you find a student committing something wrong, go and find out who the teacher is and beat him. A similar event has occurred recently with Boeing shuffling CEO and board chairman posts after the Boeing 737 Max plane disaster.[9] At the same time, we find the futility of creating an act of parliament where we have no means of measuring such clauses as that for an independent director "to uphold ethical standards of integrity and probity." Then we find society continues to be ignored in all the happenings within a corporate wall. This book brings out a scientific analysis of the Corporate Atomic Structure that provides a basis of measurement to these critical functions essential for the smooth running of an organization.

Ethics is subtler than the subtle. The COSO Framework works on the corporate entity's people. The denominator for integrity and ethical values is people. Ethics has been brought from the unknown to the known as a tangible substance. If the code for independent directors and the COSO Framework are to succeed, ethics, subtler than the subtle, has to be brought to the level of the known. The known level is of matter that is infinite in numbers. Connecting the two—the intangible, the basis of ethical values, an energy force, a constant singularity, on one side, and the tangible substance that is infinite, on the other—is indeed an exciting exercise for an intuitive mind.

The three factors of Keynes's Animal Spirits that lay stress on instability are moral, hedonistic, and economic degradation and these shall be explored further.

Keynes brings forth the cause of such degradation to these three factors, but he also suggests a way out of the chaos that corporate is entangled in.

Two key principles of Animal Spirits are "1. a spontaneous urge to action rather than inaction, 2. not as the outcome of a weighted average of quantitative benefits multiplied by quantitative probabilities."[10] Corporate needs spontaneous action, meaning action by individuals employed by a company, without exception. Quantitative data is indeed humongous. Spontaneous optimism is the catchphrase, rather than mathematical expectations. The data explosion has graduated from Kb to Mb to Gb to Tb, yet the adage remains—garbage in, garbage out. Within its own wall, a company's data becomes unreliable, for it is left with an audited balance sheet and nothing else. Polman has abandoned submitting quarterly results for Unilever, focusing on a long-term sustainability plan. Rightly so. Corporate should also look into a spontaneous action to find and replace existing quantitative data with qualitative elements of the same data. Inaction already occurs by sitting on data for too long. This has gone on for several decades now, the pathetic status quo. Corporate admires itself and is lost in the masquerade.

Knowledge is the goal of Ethics

The spontaneous urge comes from within. When James Burke, CEO of Johnson & Johnson, took such action as to reiterate an existing time-proven culture, it permeated the whole organization. An individual with such an urge could end up as a whistleblower too. Both the whistleblower as well as ethically responsible employees are for the societal good when it arises in a more mature stage of knowledge. Knowledge is the goal of ethics. Any corporate not founded in an ethical motive is wrong. Freedom of enterprise is a freedom to choose right, not wrong. It is not a choice between right and wrong. But course correction would be needed when an event goes off the trajectory, such as the introduction of cheat software.

The current news is that Bayer and BASF have been ordered to pay $265 million to a U.S. peach farmer in the Weedkiller Suit, on account of his peach orchard being destroyed. Bayer faces nearly 140 similar lawsuits in U.S. courts, plus thousands of other suits that claim health damage from Monsanto's glyphosate-based Roundup.[11]

Looking at the multibillion corporation's decisions, what is apparent is that UNCAC Article 13, Participation of Society, is absent. Public awareness is an ex post facto result, coming not from the companies but the courts of law. Now when public asks where corporate governance is, we find accountability factors just not there. This must change. For example, the Food and Drug Administration (FDA) Modernization Act of 1997, before being enacted, solicited comments from all the stakeholders, including the public, globally. FDA rules are rules, where a rule expresses the truth and when it is being certified to have been followed as prescribed, then it justifies conduct. That truth is ethics and that conduct is knowledge. Therefore, knowledge is the goal of ethics.

In the case of Volkswagen as well as of Siemens, actions they initiated after the material events, they are bound by the principle of UNCAC Article 10, Public Reporting. Society would like to confirm that such material events do not repeat. Start with a clear strategic plan for the future. Avoid the word "somehow." It is an expression of the fallibility of our market response to what we produce and sell. It need not be so. It can be precise when qualitative elements are underlined. Spontaneous optimism arises out of the qualitative elements of management. An urge to understand cheat software here, a wrong acquisition there, corrects the flow of events in the right direction. Differentiating the Boeing board and CEO functions becomes the lead indicator of delineating the duties of an organization.

Pulsating Energy

Good or bad, any outcome of operations in a company is attributed to a nonentity. It stops with quarterly or annual results in a balance sheet. A balance sheet cannot convey how vibrant such a company is. Pulsating energy is the only resource an organization, nay the planet earth, has. Our current efforts to tap solar energy as an alternate fuel warrants a moment's scrutiny of the one and the only indestructible resource—energy. At this juncture, a word about the intangible. The intangible is antimatter, and similarities exist between matter and antimatter on the one hand and the tangible and the intangible on the other. Intangible in the mundane world of business management has been used in only one instance, as intangible assets. Otherwise, unsurprisingly, it is not touched at all. Tangible on the other hand is easily defined. A physics textbook describes matter as "that which takes up space and has mass." Every physical object we have ever seen consists of matter and it is indeed tangible. The tangible is a subject corporate is closely involved with. It is with the intangible that the discomfort sets in.

Man's quest is to define and quantify this intangible. Let us examine what is antimatter and the part played by it. The experiment is on with a Large Hadron Collider (LHC), a 27-km long tunnel where beams of particles are fired to prove the theory that when a particle meets its antiparticle, they annihilate each other, and their entire mass is converted into pure energy. One of the LHC detectors, code-named LHCb, is attempting to investigate whether equal amounts of matter and antimatter were created in the Big Bang and what happened to the "missing" antimatter. When matter and antimatter come into contact, they annihilate, in a flash of energy. The Big Bang should have created equal amounts of matter and antimatter. But matter exists far more in the universe than antimatter. When antimatter collides with matter, pure energy emerges. Correspondingly, for corporate, the matter is turned into energy. There are two processes for corporate. The first is the Creative Process that turns a conceptual idea into matter. We call it innovation. The Creative Process is of many dimensions and keeps churning out what we need in every walk of corporate management. What scientists have been continuously exploring, the existence of antimatter in the known universe, corporate also needs to explore within its own domain—where the antimatter is and how it infuses energy for them.

What we see in corporate is nothing but matter, the tangible. The management of corporate affairs by virtue of visibility is matter turned around and made use of. This, the second, let us call the Action Process. All corporate processes occur under only two primal process management setups: the Creative Process and the Action Process, that is, creation and destruction. Modern physics has thus revealed that every subatomic particle not only performs an energy dance but also is an energy dance, a pulsating process of creation and destruction. Strange but true, the quicker we destroy, that is, consume what we produce, greater are the profits. All great brands are built on consumption. Both, during the Creative Process and the Action Process, energy flows from the pulsating and ends up as the non-pulsating, that is, from creation to destruction. An intellectual property right (IPR) created is an object containing non-pulsating energy that enables the accomplishment of an infinite succession of finite purposes by controlling each goal.

Corporate is governed by Newton's First Law of Motion. For the energy to flow from corporate, there must be a collision, as when antimatter collides with matter. During the Action Process, energy is multiplied by its usage. Matter—or in the corporate world, objects—attracts consumers or individuals in society to collide with it, in order to transport itself from one form to another, to go from the stages of creation to destruction. An advertising firm's revenue is based on how enticing a product looks to the consumer, and this determines how rapidly a product will travel through the cycle of creation and destruction. It is a process that abides by the fundamental laws of physics. This is better explained by Newton's First Law of Motion: "An object will remain at rest or in uniform motion in a straight line unless acted upon by an external force." For corporate, the external force is the antimatter. It resides with people, who are the repository of pulsating energy. It is up to them to kick-start the matter surrounding them, from transforming raw materials to end products directly in the consumer's hands. Just-in-time (JIT) is made simple by making subatomic particles dance all the way. If corporate wants subatomic particles to dance, the external force has to work. In nature, this force is never static. Neither is society, whether the consumers or creators within corporate. Yet, we assume that nature functions naturally and without particular effort. It is not so. The very existence of the universe depends on its continuous cycle of energy creation, in a precise and stately manner. It is possible for corporate to replicate this cycle of creation precisely as nature does, with unchallengeable benchmarks for another four-and-a-half billion years! In the case of corporate, subatomic particles tend to rest, leading to the loss of energy creation. In other words, an inactive antimatter. The principle is the same: Collide objects with pulsating energy. Simply put, make an effort to move the object from one plane to the other. Energy creation is thus the very essence of corporate affairs.

The missing antimatter should be found out. When IL&FS goes down sinking the Indian economy with it after several years of mismanagement or Volkswagen implants cheat software for over 11 million vehicles, check your premises—search for the missing antimatter. This means corporate is in a bullock-cart stage, with square wheels fitted onto the cart. We exacerbate the situation by churning out ineffective data. The data explosion has indeed been mind-boggling and inexplicable. Let us find out the corporate data explosion and compare it with the data the universe has. Carl Sagan simplified that calculation. He said the total number of stars in the universe is greater than all the grains of sand on all the beaches of the earth. Corporate data does not even count for square yard of a beach. The universe undoubtedly has infinite matter beyond a mathematical calculation. That settled, if we take a cue and recall the earlier posture toward antimatter, which was in equal measure at the time of the Big Bang, we shall surely wonder of the disappearance of antimatter from the universe. In this respect, corporate should take a cue from nature.

"The nitrogen in our DNA, the calcium in our teeth, the iron in our blood, the carbon in our apple pies were made in the interiors of collapsing stars. We are made of star-stuff," Carl Sagan said.[12] Corporate is full of people with pulsating energy and who are made up of star-stuff. The behavior pattern of corporate is no different from that of the universe. Corporate management largely ignores this and only occupies itself with objects, the tangible, matter. The subject has disappeared like antimatter whereas it is that which creates energy. It is thus worth our while to locate the antimatter within a corporate entity.

The search for antimatter within corporate reveals some stunning information. Professor of computational neuroscience at the Massachusetts Institute of Technology (MIT), Sebastung Seung says in a Technology, Entertainment and Design (TED) talk, "Your brain contains 100 billion neurons and 10,000 times as many connections." Professor of molecular cellular physiology at Stanford, Stephen Smith says of brain imaging: "In a human, there are more than 125 trillion synapses just in the cerebral cortex alone."[13] René Marois from the Center for Integrative and Cognitive Neurosciences at Vanderbilt Vision Research Center states, "The human brain is heralded for its staggering complexity and processing capacity: its hundred billion neurons and several hundred trillion synaptic connections can process and exchange prodigious amounts of information over a distributed neural network in the matter of milliseconds."[14]

Scientific analysis provides the foundation for comparison of intangible processes with tangible objects, with matter that takes up space and has mass. Astrophysicist Jayant Narlikar when asked to describe what existed before the Big Bang replied that it was beyond human imagination. That's our limitation. Limited by the three-dimensional aspect of the universe. Yet, it's so vast, impossible to figure out space and time. Matter in its form of galaxies, stars, and planets is said to add up to only 4 percent and the balance is made up of dark matter (23 percent) and dark energy

(73 percent).[15] Our human brains have that neural network functioning well in exploring space, but need to attend to exploring a corporate entity.

Spacecraft Voyager 2, launched in August 1977, provides us not only with an idea of the vastness of space but of the foresight of National Aeronautics and Space Administration (NASA) scientists. Voyager 2 has set a course for Sirius—the brightest star in the sky. It went past Jupiter in 1979, Saturn in 1981, Uranus in 1986, and Neptune in 1989, a 12-year grand journey through the solar system. Voyager 2 had already covered 16 billion km from the earth when NASA engineers sent a coded instruction to change course. Even traveling at the speed of light, the instruction took 14 hours to reach the satellite. In about 296,000 years Voyager 2 will pass 4.3 light years (25 trillion miles) from Sirius, the brightest star in the sky. The Voyagers are destined, perhaps eternally, to wander the Milky Way.[16]

Align corporate with the universal law of physics. The joke goes, during a lecture explaining the birth and death of stars, a space scientist said that "Earth would last for another 4.5 billion years." Shocked, one person got up and asked "whether the earth would disappear in 4.5 million years." The scientist replied, "No, 4.5 billion years." "Thank God, I thought it was 4.5 million years." The alarmed person sat down visibly relieved. When we deal with space, we are able to deal with a long-range planning of 296,000 years. The difference between 4.5 billion or million makes no significant difference to an individual. Yet, it does when we undertake a journey that is set and predictable. Corporate long-range planning is hardly for five years. When a mishap like a cheat software happens, the group's strategy for the year is set back by 7 years. Corporate struggles to get through a 5-year plan without a hitch. The unpredictability factors are one too many. Sustainability of elements is indeed a challenge. A long-term vision for corporate is incomprehensible while the plan for scoping the universe seems comparatively simple. Issam Sinjab, a theoretical astrophysicist, Alumni University of Leicester & University of Sussex, Department of Physics and Astronomy, has to say what Cambridge University Professor Martin Rees said when asked 'What do we mean by law of nature':

"One of Einstein's most hackneyed sayings is, 'The most incomprehensible thing about the universe is that it is comprehensible.' What Einstein meant is that the laws of nature seem to apply not just here on earth, but everywhere in the universe. We could imagine a universe where there were no laws at all, completely anarchic, every atom being different. And were that the case, we'd make no progress at all in making sense of the external world."

"The progress of science has been understanding that there are patterns in nature and discerning successive unifications of these patterns," Martin Rees says. "And this, of course, makes it possible to make predictions, which means that we don't need to remember so much—we needn't record the fall of every apple because we know how it happens."[17]

Whereas the universe functions in an organized manner within the scope of the laws of nature, corporate does the opposite. It does not conform to nature's laws. No two persons are the same. Managerial talent is attributed to the unique nature of the individual. No platform, within the laws of nature, is being created. For decades, the structure has remained the same. The platform is a unidimensional organization that runs through procurement to manufacturing to sales and every other structure. It comprises the board of directors, CEO, vice presidents. All form part of a flat organization, with all the eggs in a single basket. The results are completely anarchic. Where every individual is different, each is different in different places. In any organization, you see how each individual is governed by their own idiosyncrasies. There is no corporate goal congruence. What is comprehensible in an organization is how incomprehensible it is. Corporate must shake itself free from the "earth is as flat as a trencher" outlook.

Pins to planes, Windows to Android we have operating systems, but not for individuals. Corporate history since the Industrial Revolution has been an enormous growth in freedom of enterprise, economic prosperity, innovation, technical and intellectual advancement but it has also furthered the stoking of greed, a slow and sure decay of morality and social order culminating in high unemployment.[18] Movements such as Occupy Wall Street exemplify the recognition of this. Had the progress occurred within the framework of organic laws, it would have been far more equitable.

The science of metaphysics is an interesting subject for corporate managers. Immanuel Kant (1724–1804) raised the question of whether a science of metaphysics with a logical structure, like that of the well-established mathematical and natural sciences, was possible. That call was made nearly 300 years back. There's no attempt to sync the two. It's a materialistic world of what you see is what you get (WYSIWYG). We even have made inquiries into Shiva's abode and found an available solution. In the domain of the intangible, corporate shall search for an answer to the many mind-boggling, unpredictable human endeavors. A structured approach to understand and apply principles that would alter how we look at corporate, which has been the tangible domain of unused capability and wasted efforts. In the context of neurons and synapses that have the potential to be activated a trillion times, we are aghast to realize we occupy the dark ages, not using even a fraction of human capability.

The principle of Advaita would help in understanding the science of metaphysics. The *Brahma Sutra*[19] begins from the level of the known external feature, tangible, visible and extends to the level of the unknown. Neti, neti or na iti, na iti (not this, not this) is the rejection of whatever is known and perceived by the laws of physics. It is most difficult to know what was there before the Big Bang. By neti, neti, the cause of this universe is identified—*retrogressus ad infinitum* (the process of returning to an earlier state, again and again in the same way).[20] Retrogress to the point where everything tangible is rejected. That point is the culmination of identifying the level of energy force, from the known, phenomenal level of diversity to the unknown, non-dual, transcendental level, where there is no cause but remains the cause of all causes. That's the domain of the intangible, where there is no duality, no paradox, no plurality, and no opposite values, which are the characteristics of the tangible domain. That is a stable parameter by which the rest of the universe is calibrated. That is intangible. Corporate too is evident as pulsating energy making subatomic particles dance.

"Know Thyself"[21] was the message in the forecourt of the Temple of Apollo. It is said to be for every individual who is in pursuit of self-knowledge. In the context of corporate management, where a single company is spread over many a country, employing thousands of men and women for their business enterprise, knowledge about oneself becomes crucial for corporate development, a stable parameter by which the rest of corporate is calibrated. A wise group of companies would look into this dictum "Know Thyself" for self-governance. Having created the solar system of the sun and the moon and the planets, the universe conducts itself with the least interference. In other words, the entire universe of galaxies and cosmos[22] is self-governed. It is about time corporate understands the need for efficient and effective self-governance. Self-governance is the ultimate delegation of authority and independence. It is inevitable at a primal level.

Sebastian Seung, Evnin Professor in neuroscience, professor of computer science at Princeton Neurosciences Institute, talks of the mapping of the brain, what he calls "connectome."[23] It would take a few generations to map all the possibilities of the neuron's connectomes. David Eagleman, American neuroscientist, author, science communicator, and an adjunct professor at Stanford University, talks of the sheer number of such connections in a single brain, existing in such density that it bankrupts our language.[24] We have to invent new types of mathematics to even address this. There are so many connections between these neurons that they number in hundreds of trillions. If we take a cubic centimeter of brain tissue, there are as many connections between its neurons as there are stars in the galaxy. These strange, alien landscapes of neurons and synapses map our decision making. You are irrevocably yoked to the three pounds of tissue, the neural basis of morality and decision making, as David Eagleman refers to it. There ought to be no hesitation on the part of corporate bigwigs to "Know Thyself" as an efficacious dictum. Intrinsic self-governance by people is possible. Yes, we can—self-govern!

It is time we look for where antimatter is. That's the crux of the whole of the management operating system. In a single brain filled with neurons and synapses, there is no need to look elsewhere for missing antimatter. Carl Sagan says we are made of star-stuff. Neuroscientists say a single brain has neurons and synapses in numbers of as many atoms as there are in the universe. Perhaps we are looking for antimatter in the wrong place.

The neural basis of morality and decision making within corporate has to be given substance and mapped. The energy within each brain needs to be directed toward creating a corporate management operating system that reflects and sustains the immense potential of the brain, for use beyond profits and growth. Finding out the utilized capacity of the brain is very simple, it is zero. In other words, when the brain is inactive, the level of inactivity is 100 percent. We can compute a corresponding collective Index of Inactivity for each corporate individual. The human brain is the decision-making apparatus. We shall map its capability and guide for corporate growth. The corporate denominator becomes antimatter.

The crucial aspect of corporate management is the acknowledgment, from Socrates to Marc Benioff, of the attrition of ethical values as a constant threat to society. *Socrates had to teach the unlearned whereas Benioff has to appeal to the senses of the learned.* The learned run far more risks than the unlearned.[25] Merely professing fiduciary responsibility for the society insincerely but not being ready to avow, acknowledge, and assume the ethical responsibility to act upon, prevents a company from progressing forward. Our entire product range is toward approaching the society, attracting them with fancy advertisements and usefulness, with a customer satisfaction driver as the crux of corporate existence. Charles Ferguson's *Inside Job* is a remarkable compendium of unethical practices illustrating how learned men in high places conducted themselves, inflicting the severest injury to other people in society. Risks the learned undertakes correspond to the practices limited to senses, without conscious thoughts. Conscious reasoning would have helped them to realize the consequences of such unethical practices but alas not to be. For such people, a large majority of them, entering into a more mature stage of synthetic and intuitive knowledge does not exist. They want to remain inside Plato's cave. What we have also seen is the neuroscientists confirming the extraordinary capability every brain has. The synapses and neurons in such brains are never triggered, for they remain sluggish. The neurons and synapses to get activated need deep conscious thought, which ethical message alone offers. Moral degradation or demoralization of society's ethical structures can be repaired by reconstructing anew the rules of ethical values firmly established and put into practice.

At the same time, deconstructing the senseless practices, of instinctive habits that are truly valueless due to ethical indifference toward the society, is crucial to escape from Plato's cave. Attrition of ethical values refers to every single learned individual, as to constructing values and deconstructing valueless.

However, in our concern about the degradation of values, corporate holds the key to unraveling the economic benefits of attributing a value system to the sustainability of profits. The profit motive overtakes the ethical motive for an organization when it comes to the crunch. Corporate is not in politics but in business. Declaring the adoption of UNCAC as part of CoBP can pose many hurdles. The first motive is indeed profits, without which society gets no benefit. It is not a stand-alone exercise bereft of a value system. Efficiency brings profits but the sustainability of the value system alone maintains sustainable profits. Companies that started well with detailed anti-corruption internal rules, like SAP Software Solutions,[26] fell on the way side, arriving at a settlement with the FCPA. This is dangerous. It also means we create policies but have no inclination to follow them through. This makes it a "read, laughed and filed code" scenario. Ethical assets have to be created by a continuous check on critical control points (CCPs) on a daily basis. When so effectively operated, the value system exemplifies sustainability, which becomes evident in profits. The language corporate understands is money. Sow the value system, reap the profits. We are at the end of the tether, when auditors have joined the bandwagon of allowing, nay participating in, frauds committed by the top echelon. This book gets into the root of the matter and offers a solution to operate an effective value system.

Never in the history of mankind have so many dedicated people, as of today, served and struggled to establish a humane society around the world. These men and women, including many within the government, have relentlessly pursued transparency, human rights, anti-corruption, environmental protection, whistleblowers' protection, and right to information. Their grace on this planet, as Swami Vivekananda uttered in his famous Chicago speech, enables "the dumb eloquent and the cripple cross mountains," we shall be grateful for. For it is they who ask you: Who are you? The cosmos is within you. Nitrogen in your DNA, the calcium in your teeth, iron in your blood, everything you are made of was forged in the interiors of collapsing stars. You are made of star-stuff. You are the only pulsating energy. You have within yourself such capabilities. You trigger your antimatter. You can take corporate to the levels of accomplishments never seen before.

Who are YOU?

Chapter 2: Points to Ponder

1. Individual unleashing energy—a new form of capitalism: Paul Polman and Marc Benioff are looking for a new form of capitalism where unleashing other people's energy is highlighted as the main criterion for leadership. Their calls for change are accepted.
2. Animal Spirits—John Maynard Keynes: Marc Benioff has called upon America's top corporations to be responsible for improving society by serving all stakeholders—ethically, morally, and fairly. Keynes had forewarned the same succinctly in the last century. Keynes warning, left unmeasured, readdresses in the context of continued corporate apathy toward such bombastic ideals.
3. Indian Companies Act 2013 and the COSO Framework: The Indian Companies Act 2013, highlighting ethical standards of integrity and probity, and the COSO Framework on integrity and ethical values show how these regulatory frameworks pay lip service to ideals but are insincere as to how they are practiced, controlled, and measured. Ethics, which is subtler than the subtle, has to be brought to the known level.
4. Two key principles of Animal Spirits: (i) A spontaneous urge to action rather than inaction, (ii) not as the outcome of a weighted average of quantitative benefits multiplied by quantitative probabilities.
5. Pulsating energy: Corporate is governed by Newton's First Law of Motion. For the energy to flow from corporate, there must be a collision, as when antimatter collides with matter. That energy is the pulsating energy, the only resource an organization, nay the planet earth, has.
6. Voyager 2—vastness of space conquered: The National Aeronautics and Space Administration (NASA) measures the position Voyager 2 would be in 296,000 years from now. That is the long-range planning (LRP) NASA has taken into account. Whereas corporate LRP is just about 5 years, which corporates keep struggling with. Corporate can take a cue from NASA's planning for space administration.

7. Align corporate with laws of universe: The corporate platform—a two-dimensional flat organization structure that is practiced even now—is indeed inadequate for the challenges an organization poses. It has to go. Corporate must come out of their "earth is as flat as a trencher" outlook.
8. A Science of Metaphysics: Such a science, with a logical structure like that of the well-established mathematical and natural sciences, is made possible.
9. Principle of Advaita: This involves finding the domain of the intangible.
10. Know Thyself: This is the knowledge of one's capability leading to delegate self-governance for corporate.
11. Antimatter: Now that the antimatter is found out, the search is over in trying to locate where it is. From now on the corporate denominator is antimatter.
12. Attrition of Ethical Values: Reconstruct values and deconstruct valueless.
13. Who are you? You are intangible. You are the pulsating energy. You are the corporate denominator.

Notes

1. P. Polman, L.F. de Rothschild. May 23, 2014. "The Capitalist Threat to Capitalism." https://www.project-syndicate.org/commentary/paul-polman-and-lynn-forester-de-rothschild-call-on-companies-and-governments-to-unite-in-the-search-for-an-inclusive-and-sustainable-economy?barrier=accesspaylog.
2. D. Scialpi. 2018. "Paul Polman's Quotes about Success and Leadership — CEO of Unilever." https://medium.com/@davidescialpi/paul-polmans-quotes-about-success-and-leadership-ceo-of-unilever-52aff401a105.
3. *Inside Job*—Written by Charles Ferguson, Co-Written by Chad Beck & Adam Bolt.
4. First Post. 2019. "AgustaWestland Case: ED Links Christian Michel's Money Trail to Moser Baer, Questions Chairman Deepak Puri about 'Kickbacks'." https://www.firstpost.com/india/agustawestland-case-ed-links-christian-michels-money-trail-to-moser-baer-questions-chairman-deepak-puri-about-kickbacks-6197431.html.

5. Business Standard. 2017. "Bofors Scam: A Timeline of the 31-year-old, Rs 1,437-cr India-Sweden Deal." https://www.business-standard.com/article/current-affairs/rs-1-437-cr-india-sweden-bofors-guns-deal-timeline-of-the-31-year-old-case-117102100190_1.html.
6. OECD. "Mr. Joseph E. Murphy (Corporate Compliance and Ethics Professional)." In: *Review of the OECD Anti-bribery Instruments: Compilation of Responses to Consultation Paper*, March 31, 2008.
7. Companies Act 2013. SCHEDULE IV. [See section 149(8)]: CODE FOR INDEPENDENT DIRECTORS. Guidelines of professional conduct An independent director shall uphold ethical standards of integrity and probity.
8. S. Mcnally. 2013. "The 2013 COSO Framework & SOX Compliance." https://www.coso.org/documents/COSO%20McNallyTransition%20Article-Final%20COSO%20Version%20Proof_5-31-13.pdf.
9. N. Balu, E.M. Johnson. 2019. "Boeing Board Strips CEO of Chairman Title Amid 737 MAX Crisis." https://www.reuters.com/article/us-boeing-ceo-idUSKBN1WQ2SH?utm_campaign=trueAnthem%3A+Trending+Content&utm_content=5da13d28594d1700014c20af&utm_medium=trueAnthem&utm_source=twitter.
10. ISN ETH Zurich The General Theory of Employment, Interest, and Money By John Maynard Keynes 1366_KeynesTheoryofEmployment.pdf
11. J. Davidson. 2020. "Bayer and BASF Ordered to Pay $265 Million to U.S. Peach Farmer in Weedkiller Suit." https://www.ecowatch.com/bayer-dicamba-peach-farmer-lawsuit-2645173076.html.
12. V. Janek. 2014. "What Does It Mean To Be 'Star Stuff'?" https://www.universetoday.com/117494/what-does-it-mean-to-be-star-stuff/.
13. The Astronomist. 2011. "A Cubic Millimeter of Your Brain." http://theastronomist.fieldofscience.com/2011/07/cubic-millimeter-of-your-brain.html.
14. The Astronomist. 2011. "A Cubic Millimeter of Your Brain." http://theastronomist.fieldofscience.com/2011/07/cubic-millimeter-of-your-brain.html. Note although title is millimeter Dr. David Eagleman himself corrects it to centimeter.
15. P. Rincon. 2008. "'Big Bang' Experiment Starts Well." http://news.bbc.co.uk/2/hi/sci/tech/7604293.stm.
16. P. Baldwin. 2017. "NASA's Voyager 2 Heads for Star Sirius... by Time It Arrives Humans Will Have Died Out." https://www.express.co.uk/news/world/567957/NASA-s-Voyager-2-sets-course-for-star-Sirius-by-time-it-arrives-human-race-will-be-dead.
17. Issam Sinjab: Alumni University of Leicester & University of Sussex https://www.researchgate.net/post/A_question_on_Time_as_an_emergent_property
18. Adapted from: S. Radhakrishnan. 1939. *Eastern Religions and Western Thought*. (London, UK: Oxford University Press).

19. Nature of Upanishads: Vedas are generally considered to have two portions, viz., (1) portion dealing with action or rituals and (2) portion dealing with knowledge (http://vedicheritage.gov.in/upanishads/). *Brahma Sutra* deals with the knowledge portion, as stated in (2) above: it is a synthetic study of the Upanishads (http://sivanandaonline.org/public_html/?cmd=displaysection&section_id=578). In this book, as the reader would find later, corporate atomic structure also has only two processes: (1) Creative and (2) Action (i.e., policy and practices).
20. "Brahma Sutra—The Divine Life Society." http://sivanandaonline.org/public_html/?cmd=displaysection&section_id=597.
21. K. Best. 2018. "Know Thyself: The Philosophy of Self-Knowledge." https://today.uconn.edu/2018/08/know-thyself-philosophy-self-knowledge/#.
22. Cosmos is in the realm of "existence," where we can observe the orderly system governed by natural laws, whereas universe also "exists" but includes dark matter and dark energy, which we are unaware of as to the very existence. Cosmos adds up to only 4 percent, while the universe, which consists of dark energy and dark matter, adds up to 96 percent. Universe is everything that exists, including time and space, matter, and the laws that govern them. (Read more: "Difference Between Cosmos and Universe," http://www.differencebetween.net/science/nature/difference-between-cosmos-and-universe/#ixzz6J7d3shLY)
23. S. Seung. 2010. "I Am My Connectome – TED Talk." https://www.ted.com/talks/sebastian_seung_i_am_my_connectome?language=en.
24. D. Eagleman. 2013. "David Eagleman: Brain over Mind?" https://www.youtube.com/watch?v=UWBtT-Gl4vQ.
25. Dr. Radhakrishnan's interpretation from: Brihadaranyaka Upanishad, Ch. IV—4.10.
26. J.R. Iyer. 2011. "Index of Inactivity Measuring SAP's #Sustainability Leadership of UNGC." https://jayaribcm.wordpress.com/2011/03/30/index-of-inactivity-measuring-saps-sustainability-leadership-of-ungc/.

CHAPTER 3

Intangible Assets

We have heard a clear and consistent message on financial instruments accounting—fix this once, fix it comprehensively, and fix it in an urgent and responsible manner.

—Sir David Tweedie*

The development of the intangible asset as an accounting standard is worth a study to understand how it is defined and to overrule the damage a casual inquiry may cause. Accounting standard IAS 38, the Intangible Asset, emerged in 1998. Every accounting standard offers a clear definition of each term it refers to. IAS 38 defines intangible assets, useful life, asset, amortization, and so on, but not the word "intangible" as such. Let us find how the balance sheet was an enabled instrument, but it turned out to be otherwise after the introduction of IAS 38. Let us look into the damage IAS 38 caused accounting firms. We will also find out why the term "intangible asset" is an oxymoron. The emergence of IAS 38, compared with its original avatar IAS 9 in 1978, Accounting for Research and Development Activities, was an upgrade caused by the rapidly changing industrial scenario during the period. Let us elaborate on its significance.

Accounting standards that are currently in use are IAS 38, Intangible Assets, and IAS 36, Impairment of Assets. These are issued by the International Accounting Standards Board (IASB). The IASB was founded on April 1, 2001, as the successor to the International Accounting Standards Committee (IASC). IAS 38 offers us a definition of intangible assets: "An intangible asset is an identifiable non-monetary asset without physical substance."[1]

---

*Immediate Response to US "Unnecessary." https://www.accountancydaily.co/immediate-response-us-unnecessary

Its predecessor, IAS 9, Exposure Draft E9, Accounting for Research and Development Activities, was announced in February 1977. The resulting standard was approved for publication in March 1978. The *World Economic Survey* 1977 reports,

> The year 1977 saw a difficult economic recovery for the developed economies. High rates of unemployment were accompanied by the persistence of excess capacity in most countries, and the hopes rested on a flourishing international trade in both manufactures and agricultural products, with capacity utilization in U.S. manufacturing industry still only 83%.[2]

IAS 9, 1977, and the Year of GRACE

In 1977, when IAS 9 was being approved for publication, the global scenario was something like this: The NAVSTAR global positioning system (GPS) was being inaugurated by the United States; the first commercial Concorde flight was on its way from London to New York; NASA was successfully testing the space shuttle; Apple II was the first mass-marketed personal computer; Microsoft was a two-year-old startup; Federal Reserve year-end interest rates stood at 7.75 percent; the Dow Jones Industry Average stood at 831; oil prices after the Yom Kippur war jumped to $14.95, four times that of 1973; downsizing programs involving billions of dollars in reengineering efforts were being undertaken in the auto industry; and there was rising government pressure[3] in the United States to have fuel-efficient cars. Merger and acquisitions during the year were as follows: General Electric's $2 billion purchase of Utah International, a company that mines coal and copper. Mobil Oil acquired Marcor for $1 billion, and Atlantic-Richfield's $700 million buyout of Anaconda, the copper mining giant.

The year also witnessed the emergence of the Foreign Corrupt Practices Act (FCPA) in the United States after turbulent years on account of the Lockheed scandal. Scandals during the early 1970s triggered a peer review at Peat, Marwick, Mitchell, the audit firm of some of the companies involved and the largest of the eight major accounting firms of that time, by accounting firm Arthur Young. The review cleared Peat, Marwick, Mitchell of any misconduct.

The industry was looking for relief. Investment in R&D was seen as an absolute necessity on the one hand, with the concern that the expenses for it were eating into profits, on the other. During the discussion stage of the exposure draft (Exposure Draft E9, Accounting for Research and Development Activities) this was very evident. Many industries were feeling the pinch on costs eroding profits with no corresponding asset growth. Particularly affected was the aerospace industry in the United Kingdom. Yielding to pressure, the IASC issued a new exposure draft, ED 17, in April 1976. This required capitalization of development expenditures in certain cases. E9 was made final with minor changes as IAS 9 in March 1978. Further, in December 1993, the standard was renamed "IAS 9 Research and Development Costs."

The UN *World Economic Survey* report of 1977, under the introduction "Disquieting International Trends," stated,

> There is a widespread uncertainty and unease about prospects for the world economy in the next several months and even a longer time span... It is primarily on an acceleration of productive investment activity that most of these countries are counting to reestablish a steady rate of growth; but the slow expansion of both domestic and external demand, coupled with the external uncertainties generated by exchange instability and protectionist tendencies, have discouraged new investment.[4]

With the rising pressure on industry to search for new avenues for production, the heavy investment in R&D, and a far from optimal industrial climate, it was natural for the industry to approach IASC. As an organization, IASC had seen several such deliberations and brought about a coordinated and inclusive approach to publishing the Generally Accepted Accounting Principles (GAAP). In 1977, it did this for IAS 9 R&D Activities.

Accounting firms had a grip over corporate affairs that can be summarized under the following five issue areas.

44   CORPORATE CITIZENSHIP AND SUSTAINABILITY

G-R-A-C-E

Governance

IAS 9, the instrument by which governance could be administered by the audit profession, stood up to the pressure. It was a commendable role IASC played over the years. The balance sheet had come to be relied upon as the most reliable record of activities transacted by individual companies globally.

Responsibility

Setting a precedent for taking responsibility, audit firm Peat, Marwick, Mitchell undertook the responsibility of clearing their name by appointing Arthur Young for the peer review of their auditing practices.

Authority

Industry was made aware that they had no other recourse than to get the approval from professional accounting bodies through published accounting standards for any inclusion or change of balance sheet items. This meant that a journal entry at the corporate level needed prior approval from the accounting governing body. Governance was at its best. The industries looking for approval for capitalization of R&D costs, be it aerospace, pharmaceuticals, automobile, hardware, were all for an end product that was a tangible item. Accounting firms armed with IAS 9 would have had no difficulty in verifying the product as well as the costs related to the R&D capitalization. IAS 9 had emerged after due diligence.

Credibility

Arthur Young, another major auditing firm, had gained the trust of society to audit the practices of another major firm. Society was naturally agitated over the several scandals that erupted during that period, forcing an FCPA to emerge.

Enabled Balance Sheet

It was at this time that the balance sheet emerged as an enabled instrument.

The year 1995, IAS 38, and the year of Nick Leeson: Looking ahead to 1995, when Exposure Draft E50 Intangible Assets was introduced, the year witnessed a boom in technology. The most reliable investment opportunities were in American Online (AOL) for the Internet, Micron Technology for semiconductors, Motorola for hardware, and Microsoft for software. The year also saw a Dutch firm, ING, buying up Baring PLC for a nominal amount of $1.60, after one individual, Nick Leeson, barely 28, brought down the bank with reckless gambling and speculation on the Tokyo Stock Exchange. He lost $1.3 billion, making the 220-year-old bank insolvent. It was also the year when Paul Allen invested $500 million in DreamWorks, the film studio founded by Steven Spielberg and two others. The U.S. space shuttle docked with Russian Mir space station for the first time. The year-end Dow Jones Industrial Average stood at 5117, oil prices were $16.75 average, and Microsoft Windows 95 and Internet Explorer were released.

In 1995, Boutros Boutros-Ghali, who was UN secretary-general, reading the *World Economic and Social Survey*, stated,[5]

> At a time when the global economy is comparatively healthy, many regions are enjoying increasing prosperity and show an ability to sustain their growth: Simultaneously, for many of the world's citizens, this is an era of hardship—and worse suffering seems to lie ahead. In a world that is tightly linked economically, this imbalance threatens the long-term welfare of both developed and developing economies—this survey poses fundamental questions about our priorities and our commitment to the future.
>
> Commenting on the exchange rate crisis,
>
> creditor Governments and financial community, including investors who lost considerable sums in the wake of the crisis, have asked whether better international surveillance of domestic policy might avert future crises. This is a question about information, analysis and the politics of policymaking; it is a complicated question that does not yet seem to have a clear answer.[6]

In this global context, 1995 also saw the introduction of exposure draft E50 for Intangible Assets. The stage was set to adopt new policies on changing the industrial scene. When IAS 9 Accounting for R&D activities was introduced in 1977, the emphasis was on products leaning toward blue-collared employment-oriented industries. By 1995, when the demand for a fresh look had arisen, the emphasis had shifted considerably toward brands, software, copyrights, patents, and so on. Dr Herve L. Stolowy and Dr Axel Haller, in their article on ED50 Intangible Assets,[7] write about what transpired during the discussion stage. The primary concern was somehow to recognize brands as an asset so that their balance sheets would look healthier. At the same time, the fundamental problems faced to define intangible to move forward for publishing an accounting standard were evident, as the exposure draft defined intangible assets as identifiable, nonmonetary assets without physical substance. In European countries, such as France, the General Accounting Plan (Plan Comptable General, PCG) 1982 (CNC, 1986: I.33) defines intangible assets as being fixed assets other than tangible or financial assets. A fixed asset here is defined as an asset acquired for long-term use in the operation of the business. Therefore, intangible assets are only recognized by comparison with tangible assets, which correspond to real rights over tangible objects. However, the purpose was obvious: to know whether brands can be recognized in the balance sheet. In August 1997, IASC modified E50, which was reexposed as Exposure Draft E59 Intangible Assets. Finally, IAS 38 Intangible Assets was published in September 1998. This was a watershed definition of the role of governing bodies in the accounting profession.

IAS 38 defines intangible assets as an identifiable nonmonetary asset without physical substance. Further, IAS 38 outlines the identifiability and recognition criteria. The urgency with which industry needed to recognize intangible assets was quite palpable in the changing scenario.

The year 1995, which saw the beginning of the tussle between hardware and software technology, could be termed as the year of Windows 95 and Nick Leeson, for better or worse. During the year there were disturbing reports on brand-related initial public offerings (IPOs), with several warnings filed with the U.S. Securities and Exchange Commission (SEC) but hidden from private placement memorandum. Offshore tax havens were used liberally to establish companies without disclosing the ownership information while filing the court papers. The *World Economic and Social Survey* 1995 made a chilling statement:

> Traditionally, the major financial intermediaries have been fractional—reserve banks and thrifts, whose assets and liabilities are, except in bankruptcy, redeemable at par. The assets and liabilities are not directly traded on secondary markets and hence are not "marked to market." In other words, the "prices of loans and deposits on the banks" books are always at par, notwithstanding interest rate changes… If the market's share of total finance were small, this would not matter but traditional par-value banking is gradually being eclipsed by the so-called share of "mutual fund" banking which deals only in securitized assets.[8]

The erosion of balance sheet assets had already begun in 1995. Further, the urgency of inflating the balance sheet figures has been a dominant factor.

> During the discussion stage of E50 (Intangible Assets), brand value is used as a tangible asset was quite apparent. Because of this importance of brands for the economic development of certain businesses, the accounting treatment of brands has been a matter of debate and controversy in many countries, such as Australia and the United Kingdom for instance, where companies, such as Grand Metropolitan and Rank Hovis McDougall, decided in 1988 to include the value of brand names, either purchased or internally developed, in their consolidated Balance Sheets.[9]

It shall be noted, the use of the intangible asset in a balance sheet was 10 years ahead of official release. The definition, therefore, becomes a crucial aspect of governance.

Asset is a tangible item with a specific useful life attached to it, but the very term "intangible" means everlasting and imperishable. IAS 38 defines all used terms, such as useful life, asset, amortization, as they all are in business parlance at the time of publication. All except one, "intangible." Perhaps they meant "invisible" instead. An intangible asset is an oxymoron. Intangible is antimatter and an asset is matter. They are opposite poles.

The intangible asset was the first licensed clearance for breaking the age-old par-value banking. Mutual funds were vehicles to invest in "tangible asset-based vehicles" but with the emergence of non-bank financial system, mutual funds started investing in companies that had more intangible packaged assets with inflated value in every step of the value chain.

During the financial crisis of 2008, Timothy Geithner, then president and CEO of the Federal Reserve Bank in New York, said, "The scale of long-term risky and relatively illiquid assets financed by very short-term liabilities made many of the vehicles and institutions in this parallel financial system vulnerable to a classic type of run."[10]

There was an urgent need to assess the future economic benefits of such assets. Hence, IAS 36 Impairment of Assets was published on July 1, 1999. An asset is impaired when its carrying amount exceeds its recoverable amount. However, if IAS has been following a strict chronological system, impairment must have influenced an intangible asset to emerge with a handicap.

The purpose of international accounting standards is "to develop IFRS® Standards that bring transparency, accountability, and efficiency to financial markets around the world. Our work serves the public interest by fostering trust, growth, and long-term financial stability in the global economy."[11] What really emerges out of the standards is a. auditors' responsibility and b. public perception of or confidence in the balance sheet. As a going concern, auditors are fairly protected, which is not the case when a major scandal breaks out. Society naturally questions how and why the auditors did not ferret it out. Intellectual property, for example, could be a matter of dispute if the individual who created it challenges ownership. The valuation of an intangible asset could be one figure for the balance sheet purposes but could be a highly padded up figure for a private equity investor. In such cases, risks associated with internally generated intangible assets could be high. Purchased intangible asset is an asset generated out of a transaction where the market would decide the price, taking into consideration the risk factors and future economic benefits. It is not the case with an internally generated intangible asset.

It has a sting in the tail that was not deliberated threadbare during the exposure drafts discussions or at the review stage of IAS 38. The conditions are entirely different in capitalization between 1977 and 1995. There was no need to displace IAS 9 and substitute with IAS 38, enlarging the scope of assets covered. Such intangible assets could have remained or made use of, as off–balance sheet assets, without bringing them into the books of accounts. Even now, strictly an intellectual property right (IPR) is a work-in-progress and gets validated only if a patent is obtained. The balance sheet must be fortified to exclude non-transactional entries. The balance sheet is a simpleton, like a foolish or gullible person, ready to accept what one offers. One can't keep adding frivolous ideas to it hoping that accounting standards would help remove inconsistencies. Inventory accounting also has several methods of valuation. Select one and keep it simple. Leave the balance sheet alone.

It is not the responsibility of an accounting governing body to accommodate any industry, which is a state subject. That could create a conflict of interest by which incentives and concessions to promote a favored industry could emerge from time to time, although some professors look upon it favorably. "Knowledge-based assets make up a growing proportion of economic valuation, but people believe that current accounting models really don't capture their worth," says Wharton accounting professor David F. Larcker. "For example, despite the fact that (a company) may have intellectual property (IP) that holds significant value, the IP may not, in fact, have ever been cataloged or identified."[12] Even so, it is not on the accounting profession to accommodate such assets, which are misused by unscrupulous many.

The balance sheet is an instrument meant for transactional entries that attempts to put in the off–balance sheet entries to be avoided. The problem is, the balance sheet has become the only instrument all stakeholders, including society, depend upon. The balance sheet is no longer a trustworthy document, despite adding accounting standards upon accounting standards to justify its continuity. We need to wean off dependence on the balance sheet and create one trustworthy document everyone can rely on. Balance sheet analysis is a waste of time.

Sir David Tweedie, IASB chairman at the time of constituting the Financial Crisis Advisory Group (FCAG), said, "We have heard a clear and consistent message on financial instruments accounting—fix this once, fix it comprehensively, and fix it in an urgent and responsible manner."[13] It is doubtful. There is a fundamental flaw in the financial instrument, for it is limited by quantitative elements whereas qualitative elements go beyond auditors' scrutiny. This is beyond the comprehension of any stakeholder.

It is management's responsibility: The accounting firms that commented upon the consultation paper "Consultation Paper Review of the OECD Instruments on Combating Bribery of Foreign Public Officials in International Business Transactions Ten Years after Adoption" said, "It is management's responsibility, with the oversight of those charged with Governance, to ensure that the entity's operations are conducted in accordance with laws and regulations. The responsibility for the prevention and detection of non-compliance rests with management."[14] The audit inadequacy lies in the type of material events that are not transparent. Responsibility is shirked and the perpetrators go scot-free. Big firms have not glorified themselves by having management acknowledge responsibility, be it ethical or fiscal. They remain clueless in deciphering what's happening within the four walls of the management, though not for a want of good intentions.

A conference proposal paper says[15]:

> In fact, it is not clear that the so-called GAAP standard is even particularly meaningful anymore: companies continue to search for beneficial ways in which to disclose information about themselves with or without formal sanction... Nakamura estimated the value of U.S. gross investments in intangibles in 2000 to be at least $1 trillion annually. More recently, Corrado and Hulten (2010) estimate that in 2007, by omitting investments in intangibles, $4.1 trillion was excluded from published national accounts data in the U.S.

Big firms excuse themselves when companies keep asking for greater disclosure of their capability. It's not their failure alone but that of the accounting profession in neglecting to create a robust instrument. The millennium merger of AOL takeover of Time Warner is a case in point, creating a $335 billion company, proving that in a world ruled by finance, intangible assets rather than real assets are the indicator of real wealth. What's true in such a scenario is that the real finance is completely mopped up by speculative enterprise, a privileged area of the government notwithstanding, denying the much-needed funds for priority spending, globally. Intangible asset is indeed a croupier's delight.

G-R-A-C-E 2

To summarize the trend during this period, in 1995, intangible assets came into a period that we may call G-R-A-C-E Version 2.

Governance

The audit profession lost its control of governance over the accounting standard on account of IAS 38 being published without the keyword being defined.

Responsibility

The Big 4 firms shirked responsibility and meekly told the OECD that it was management's responsibility, the blame for oversight belonging to those charged with governance. The age-old dictum the auditor relies on to say we are a watchdog, not a bloodhound, is highly questionable, for the demands for scrutiny of corporate affairs have gone much beyond mere audit of books of accounts. The duties of the watchdog need to be thoroughly analyzed, on account of the rapid change effected by the multivarious functions of management that are qualitative.

Authority

From 1988, the industry tried to rule over the balance sheet that the audit profession lost its hold on, on account of IAS 38. In 2007, this led to the omitting of investments in intangibles, and $4.1 trillion was excluded from published national accounts data in the United States. The audit profession had become irrelevant.

Credibility

In 1977 Peat, Marwick, Mitchell took on responsibility and called upon another major firm, Arthur Young, to conduct a peer review of their auditing methodology. Today it has become the story of "He that is without sin among you, let him first cast a stone." There's no audit firm without a blemish. The audit profession after IAS 38 has lost its credibility as it now allows "management" to decide on journal entries.

Erosion of Balance Sheet

There was no hole in the balance sheet in 1977. By 1998, craters have been normalized. Excluding $4.1 trillion from published national accounts data in the United States is crater enough. The audit profession has lost its identity.

Chapter 3: Points to Ponder

1. In 1977 IAS 9 Research and Development Costs was introduced.
2. The Global Scenario around that period, economic recovery continued to be difficult in developed economies. The effect of oil prices after the Yom Kippur war was evident with downsizing programs involving billions of dollars in reengineering efforts ever undertaken in the auto industry.
3. At the same time, like before and after, corruption was corroding the nations, and the United States came out with the FCPA. Such Acts, as before and after, have failed miserably in containing such issue areas society demands to disconnect.
4. Pressure on the IASC for the purpose of capitalization of development costs was a genuine request as many industries were feeling the pinch on costs eroding profits with no corresponding asset growth. But corporate obsession toward profits, as the only means of convincing the stock market, bereft of any value system sustainability, continued unchallenged. Companies like Enron, WorldCom, Toshiba showed they are not the exceptions but are the rule among corporate buccaneers.
5. Summarizing, G-R-A-C-E [governance, responsibility, authority, credibility, and enabled balance sheet] of the audit profession was quite satisfactory through the 1990s. Thanks to the professional support and guidance IAS 9 Research and Development Costs standards provided, regulating and protecting the interests of the profession.

6. In comparison, 1995 events, when IAS 38 Intangible Assets was set to be introduced, changed the scenario in favor of corporate gaining control over the balance sheet while the audit profession simultaneously lost its.
7. The tussle between technology and technology led a 220-year bank to bankruptcy while the auditors of Baring Bros stood stupefied at the technological advancement of derivatives that they had no clue of whatsoever.
8. Auditors by G-R-A-C-E-2 remain and continue to remain graceless.

Action Points

1. Reinstate IAS 9 and scrap IAS 38.
2. Scrap the requirement for a statutory auditor. No need for a watchdog. Corporate shall self-govern and self-declare; would help investors better, to be more careful.
3. How to treat and measure a nonmonetary asset without physical substance shall be looked into.
4. The irony is that IAS 38, as Accounting Standard in 1998, had made all ethical standards ineffective and nonfunctional. Ethical standards had gone for a toss. Restore ethical standards ASAP.

Notes

1. International Accounting Standards Board. "IAS 38 Intangible Assets."
2. Department of International Economic and Social Affairs. 1978. *World Economic Survey, 1977* (New York, NY: United Nations). E/1978/70/Rev.1: ST/ESA/82.
3. The crisis also prompted a call for individuals and businesses to conserve energy—most notably a campaign by the Advertising Council using the tag line "Don't Be Fuelish" (https://www.cs.mcgill.ca/~rwest/wikispeedia/wpcd/wp/1/1973_oil_crisis.htm).
4. Department of International Economic and Social Affairs. *World Economic Survey, 1977*, p. 1—Introduction—Disquieting International Trends.
5. Department for Economic and Social Information and Policy Analysis. 1995. *World Economic and Social Survey, 1995* (New York, NY: United Nations). E/1995/50/ST/ESA/243, Preface.

6. Ibid., p. 5.
7. H.L. Stolowy, A. Haller. 1996. "Accounting for Brands in ED50 of IASC (Intangible Assets) Compared with French and German Practices—An Illustration of the Difficulty of International Harmonization." Presented at the *19th Annual Congress of the European Accounting Association Bergen*, Norway, May 2–4, 1996, p. 3.
8. Department for Economic and Social Information and Policy Analysis. *World Economic and Social Survey, 1995*, pp. 77–78.
9. H.L. Stolowy, A. Haller. "Accounting for Brands," p. 7.
10. T.F. Geithner. 2008. "Reducing Systemic Risk in a Dynamic Financial System." https://www.newyorkfed.org/newsevents/speeches/2008/tfg080609.html.
11. IFRS mission statement. https://www.ifrs.org/.
12. Knowledge@Wharton. February 13, 2002. "Valuing the Invisible: How to Manage Bankruptcies of Knowledge-based Companies."
13. P. Smith. 2009. "Immediate Response to US 'Unnecessary.'" https://www.accountancydaily.co/immediate-response-us-unnecessary.
14. OECD. 2008. "Review of the OECD Anti-Bribery Instruments: Compilation of Responses to Consultation Paper." http://www.oecd.org/daf/anti-bribery/anti-briberyconvention/40773471.pdf.
15. Athena Alliance. 2011. "Global Competition and Collaboration." In: *New Building Blocks for Jobs and Economic Growth: Intangible Assets as Sources of Increased Productivity and Enterprise Value*. http://www.oecd.org/sti/inno/48918196.pdf.

CHAPTER 4

Intangible Defined

Absence of evidence is not evidence of absence.

—Martin Rees*

Bernard Lawrence Madoff, serving a sentence for defrauding his clients of billions of dollars, is a paradox. Duping a customer base, some of them the elderly, with Ponzi schemes, he made himself $65 billion[1] and earned himself a sentence of 150 years in prison, with restitution of $170 billion. He is unlikely to fulfill either term. Good intentions should translate to better performances instead of broken promises. It should be simple enough. "Earth provides enough to satisfy every man's needs, but not every man's greed," Mahatma Gandhi said. We have to ask ourselves whether aphorisms like these are mere catchwords or can we pragmatically implement them. In an enterprise run with only a balance sheet, greed can never be stopped. Systems to control such greed, like the Committee of Sponsoring Organizations of the Treadway Commission (COSO) and the Sarbanes–Oxley Act (SOX), are handicapped by the lack of a good management operating system. Standard operating procedures (SOPs) for these systems within a company should be there to operate on, clearly indicating the policy objectives. Simply put, they are matter waiting to turn into energy. A policy document like the FCPA to turn into energy will have to be in place with a SOP and acted upon. Someone has to take the necessary steps to do it, for it does not happen organically. Ask, whether there is a need for third-party intervention and assurance by an external consultant or a do-it-yourself (DIY) kit is preferable. Understanding the intangible helps to resolve the paradox of being perfect and imperfect at the same time. Inspirational catchwords need careful scrutiny in the context of corporate governance.

---

*https://quoteinvestigator.com/2019/09/17/absence/#note-436457-8

Search for the Intangible

The objective in searching for the intangible is to decipher and buttonhole its role. It is the only energy force that both creates a mass and converts the mass into pure energy. The accomplishment of this, which we shall call the Creative Process, exemplifies in individuals what we have defined as innovation. It further assists individuals to accomplish an infinite succession of finite purposes. It does so by controlling each goal with a unique Action Process. The intangible is the pulsating energy behind all human effort.

Opposite Values

The truth is inevitably paradoxical; it contains opposite values. A dilemma exists because of the truth. That is why the truth is illogical. A logical conclusion is the most natural and inevitable outcome that can be organically derived. As such, it does not have an opposite. Beliefs, on the other hand, are polarized. The proponent of one school of thought makes a claim and an opponent from the other school raises objections to the claim. What one believes in with great conviction, the other has diametrically opposite views on. However, one does not approach nature looking for contradictions, but for symmetry. So also, in governance, a consensus is sought in advance, allowing for the objections and arguments laid in support of these objections recorded, before a policy statement is issued. A policy statement expresses the truth and justifies conduct, one in the Creative Process while preparing the set of rules and another performing during the Action Process abiding by the rules. A policy statement must be a substance of quality and action integrated.

The UNCAC is a great document that emerged after several exposure drafts and deliberations and was arrived at with consensus. However, these laws are designed as the cat's claws and teeth: benevolent to the kitten but malevolent to the rat. Truth involves completely opposite values; only then, can it be Truth. Vacuum is a space with the absence of matter but can only be explained by the matter surrounding it. Nonexistence is relative to existence. Both of them coexist in the same plane—matter. This is the law of nature. Nature is symmetrical. Thus, the opposite values give us a clue to the location of the intangible. To illustrate, let us look at a simple equation.

When $X^2 = 4$, what is X? $X = \sqrt{4}$, going further, $\sqrt{4} = ?$ $\sqrt{4} \equiv \pm 2$.

Here, $\equiv$ is a symbol with three dashes meaning "identically equal to." Without this symbol, $\equiv$, the equation is incorrect. In this equation, X acquires two values that are not just equal but identically equal to +2 as well as −2. X acquires two opposite values that are not opposed to each other. They exist in the same plane. $\pm$ are two aspects of a single movement, like a pendulum. It could be at one end and in the next moment, at the other. When we stand at the equator and look at the North Pole and the South Pole, they seem so far apart. Yet, seen from the moon, it is no different from a coin having two sides: the head and the tail. Poles apart, true, but the earth remains a single indivisible unit. Genghis Khan and Gandhi are in the same plane but remain outcomes of a single species with differing values. The left hand and the right hand are part of a single inseparable unit. Truth always counterbalances opposite values, and only then can it be the whole truth.

Study of Opposite Values

The intangible needs to be located, buttonholed, and isolated and only then can identification start. Opposite values give us a clue to its location. Illustratively, "I used to smoke 40 cigarettes a day, now I don't." There is something missing from this statement. When the same person is found smoking a few minutes later, he may reply, "I used to smoke 40 cigarettes earlier, but now I smoke 45 a day." The statement has an inherent shortcoming. An inference would, at best, confirm that the person doesn't seem to be a nonsmoker. If the person was to communicate clearly, he would have to say, "I used to smoke 40 cigarettes a day, now I have given up smoking." In the statement, "I used to smoke 40 cigarettes a day, now I don't and now I have given up smoking," the part of the sentence "given up smoking" provides clarity for the opposite value. Smoking is one end of the value and giving it up is at the other end of the value chain. Both actions require the same characteristic—effort. The action of smoking needs an effort to complete the process. Giving up smoking voluntarily, when the cigarette is easily available, requires an effort on the part of the individual. Hence, effort is the primary force that changes the action in either way, whether that's a Madoff or a Gandhi. Hence, to identify the quality of the characteristic of the substance under scrutiny, it is crucial to ferret out the character of the individual. Conduct comes later during the Action Process. Character is identifiable during the Creative Process. It shapes individuals as a substance of quality and action. Identifying the right persons for the implementation of the UNCAC, COSO, and SOX Framework, independent directors and so on within a company, the character of an individual has necessarily to be noted.

To Quote the Sage of Kanchi[2]

Our sastras give a clear idea of arthapatti through an illustration. 'Pino Devadatto diva na bhunkte.' What does the statement mean? 'The fat Devadatta doesn't eat during daytime.' Though Devadatta does not eat during the daytime, he still remains a fat fellow. How? We guess that he must be eating at night. There is something contradictory about an individual not eating and still not being thin. Here arthapatti[3] (presumption) helps us discover the cause of Devadatta being fat. Our guess that he eats at night does not belong to the category of anumana[4] (inference). To make an inference there must be a hint or clue in the original statement itself. There must be a "linga" (form or a symbol) like smoke from fire, thunder from clouds. Here there is no such linga.[5]

Auditors can no longer help themselves with the excuse, it is management's responsibility. Dig deep into the subject with the motto "absence of evidence is not evidence of absence." Opposite values help us identify the misfeasance of individuals and locate conflicts of interest, personal or professional, and of conscience. The opposite values principle can be applied to incidences such as the Rajat Gupta case. When applied to Rajat Gupta's case, the opposite values could bring out the truth. A paradox can only be resolved by diminishing imperfection in one case or increasing perfection in the other, for which you may refer and apply this principle on the case study. Who is the insider trader: Rajat Gupta, Rajaratnam, Goldman Sachs, or Warren Buffett?[6]

An Effort Transforms Mass into Energy

Cigarette smoking or nonsmoking is an Action Process. Hence effort is apparent. The phrase, "Now I don't" refers to an action, but without clarity. This clarity is corrected by the phrase "given up smoking." The pairs of opposites—heat and cold, pain and pleasure, gain and loss, victory and defeat—have certain values identified with the senses. It could take either mental or physical effort to feel it. The human mind is not capable of knowing what it was before the Big Bang when such pure energy was produced, of antimatter and matter in equal proportion. What we can know, however, is that the effort that produced the universe after the Big Bang is a Creative Process.

In the Action Process, effort is related to matter and is hence identifiable. In our example, this would be "given up smoking." In the Creative Process, effort is not identifiable in an output of matter as it is an intangible. Thus, we may surmise, the Creative Process of the universe is related to antimatter. Effort is taken to collide with matter to form pure energy. However, we are able to locate this effort and energy through innovation. The Theory of Relativity is an example of the Creative Process of the human mind, attributable to the effort of Albert Einstein. Yet, the efficient cause responsible for the theory to materialize, which made Einstein unique, is not identifiable. In Action Process, one becomes two having opposite values, whereas in Creative Process, two becomes one with antimatter colliding with intellect to create pure energy. Intellect is the cause of man-made substances. In the case of the universe, that point is the culmination of identifying the level of energy force, from the known, phenomenal level of diversity to the unknown, non-dual, transcendental level. That point, where there is no cause but remains the cause of all causes, is the domain of intangible. Here, there is no duality, no paradox, no plurality, and no opposite values, which are the characteristics of the tangible domain.

The human brain retains the power of decision making during the Creative Process as well as during the Action Process. The human brain makes of its own volition the decision to think, to produce a Substance of Quality and Action, and act upon it, with effort. That effort is intangible. The opposite value of eating is not hunger, but fasting. The option is made available to the individual to eat or give it up. To the individual it is the same effort, eating or fasting, with the values being different. They are identical. Consider it more deeply, and the opposite value of hunger is not eating, but morality. This is the contrast between a festive day on which one chooses to fast and other ordinary days. In the first instance, foregoing eating is a personal choice, whereas seeing a hungry man but not feeding him is the choice made by the society one lives in. A humane society is the one that does not allow a man to go hungry, whereas in the society one lives in today, the responsibility is left to the individual and not taken up by the state. Opposite values of hunger and morality do exist and will exist, so long a humane society or a government for the people is not formed. A hungry man knows no taste or discrimination but a man with no morality knows no fear or shame. By a study of effort, the intangible makes itself known loud and clear.

Measuring the intangible therefore will make clear to us where an individual or a society or a state stands. The formation of a humane society is the result of the Action Process. What it represents is the Action on the Quality with which the Substance is designed to deliver. It satisfies Newton's Third Law of Motion, creates the substance of Quality, and acts upon it.

Creative and Action Processes—Proof of Knowledge

Out of the six characteristics of existence, the first three—Substance, Quality, and Action— have a profound impact on the opposite values. Machinery uses precision. Human beings do not, by comparison. Action in machinery is calibrated to a high degree of efficiency, whereas in the case of an individual, action is dynamic and unpredictable. Additionally, Association, Difference, and the Inherence of an individual impact the first group (Substance, Quality, and Action). Action that is triggered becomes variable and the Quality changes, for good or bad, for a human being. The Substance that is an individual, therefore, becomes unpredictable. This is why at one time you have a Gandhi and at another, Genghis Khan. Action is thus the focal point of hazard analysis and critical control point (HACCP) in matter. It affects the Substance of the tangible. Action is the result of effort, an exertion of power or force, a source of energy. This energy is produced because of the collision between Substance in the tangible field and Effort from the intangible field. When there is no collision, it means the intangible field is in a state of inactivity and the tangible field is at rest. In such a state, an individual is at rest, comfortable, observing the happenings around the world, maybe even watching atrocities being committed, but not interfering. As Bess Myerson says, "The accomplice to the crime of corruption is frequently our own indifference." The Substance is yet to be formed as Quality, that is, morality is yet to create Substance within. This state requires a fire to annihilate greed and corruption. That fire is Effort. The opposite value of Action is thus not inaction, but alternate action. The Effort is the essence of triggering action in the tangible field and in itself, it is the intangible. The Effort is the one that possesses the elemental, undifferentiated stuff of mind and matter, connecting the intangible to the tangible.

Intangible defined: Like an athletic event is performed on a sports field, governance and management quality are all performed in the tangible field. Sportspersons who participate in the event put in efforts to accomplish the task at hand. So do the participants in the tangible field of governance. The tasks are well defined, goals are set, critical factors are arrived at, measured by the performance criteria, enabling the accomplishment of an infinite succession of finite purposes by controlling each goal. It's a complex coordination made simple when the intangible is aligned. Action Process is the one that gives such an impression since action is attributed to a single individual and the related effort put in. However, the tasks of Action Process function to a finite purpose. They are repetitive and boring ultimately. It's like a child's bedtime story: One bird comes in and picks a grain and flows away. Another bird comes in and picks a grain and flows away. Ad infinitum. Corporate ability is not questioned, but they are doing the same thing again and again. Instead of challenging competition, the tendency is to kill it. Innovation will get a big boost. Brand names will be rendered redundant when a shift toward MSMEs occurs. For products that are truly in the cottage industry sector, what is important is certification like HACCP, not a brand name. Customer focus and satisfaction would be on assurance of quality. To achieve this, the Creative Process is crucial. What is crucial for corporate is to bring the abstractions into reality, acknowledge value where value is due, and deconstruct what is valueless. Instead of doing this they constantly work toward increasing their profits. They have created a two-dimensional flat organization, picking up single grains with a single repetitive movement.

Spreadsheet Organization Structure: Corporate structure is based on what is convenient and measurable. Functioning on this principle, a basic business survived with a petty clerk keeping a single-entry bookkeeping. As transactions multiplied, it necessitated a double-entry bookkeeping. Then business grew to accommodate several departments and branch accounting. Several columns arose to keeping track of these multiple transactions, ensuring a trial balance was created for every debit and credit. Corporate structure grew in the same manner. Then it stopped. Nonfinancial material events are not part of a measuring device. The need never existed. Material events are noted but never measured. Several committees are formed mandatorily or in an ad hoc fashion but never measured. Corporate structure that stops with that is merely a spreadsheet corporate structure. Innovation for corporate remains that which can be patented and pursued to gain sales and market. What is really required is innovation in management. The cheat software was the creation of a single brain that was put into millions of vehicles. It overruled Volkswagen's self-proclaimed vision of an extraordinary value system and corporate governance and cost the company $33.6 billion. Siemens is said to have made an excellent Substance of Code of Conduct with Quality. But it had no Action. It became a "read, laughed and filed code," as the OECD anti-bribery Report[7] reveals.

You can see what neuroscientists mean when they speak of the underutilized potential of the human brain. The intangible can be used to create something beyond sales and marketing. That requires a Creative Process at its best. Try. Make an Effort.

Intangible is

1. an effort,
2. a force applied for a specific task, creative as well as action,
3. having an identifiable goal,
4. enabled by the factors for the task accomplishment, and
5. measured by defined performance criteria.

The Implication

1. The gems strung together may vary in color and species, but the supporting string is the same all through. i. Matter is a substance with the substratum of Quality and Action whether sentient or insentient with the identifiable nature of the force applied to it. That force is the effort revealing all by itself.
2. The Substance makes itself known by its Quality, through the Creative Process triggered by effort. i. Substance is not known as Substance until it acquires its inherent quality in its completed form. Every Substance has specific criteria built-in and each of them has huge energy released by the Action Process.
3. Where matter exists, so does energy. i. The one that brings it out in its entirety is the Action Process when task accomplishment takes place.
4. The study of the supporting string reveals the different shades of colors of the gems. i. Substance varies but Quality and Action are inseparably related to the Substance under study.
5. Quality and Action have a common thread, even if Substance is sentient or insentient. (i) "The living knew themselves just sentient puppets on God's stage," says T.E. Lawrence. Einstein, on the other hand, extended the argument, feeling confident that God did not play dice with the world. The physical structure of Substance is made up of the six stages of development. (i) Substance, although insentient by itself, gets the distinctiveness by clinging to the sentient. In articulation, the part that the consonant plays clinging to the vowel is analogous to the function of the Substance. Again, the origin and function of the skin of a fruit are analogous to the part that Substance plays in the phenomenon, (ii) with the aid of Quality and Action of Substance, the sentient reveals itself. The sentient is a Substance like a police or military force, as much as insentient that may be a constitution, written laws, an IPR, or accounting standards.
6. An object or a phenomenon exhibits certain symmetry performing the given operations consistently on all parts. i. When the Substance misbehaves against the standards set in by Quality inherent to it, the Action Process finds the predetermined task accomplishment difficult to achieve. This could be due to either the distortion in the

Quality of the Substance or the inactive operations in the Action Process.
7. It is the intangible that makes the Substance function, and that functioning is Governance.
8. Sentient Substance does lose its Quality by lack of Governance and so does the insentient Substance. i. A systematic observation of the stage where the Substance stays at any point of time reveals the state of affairs of governance as a whole.
9. Discovering the truth is an intellectual effort.

Chapter 4: Points to Ponder

1. Search for intangible leads to resolve many a paradox.
2. Opposite values refine to acknowledge the existence of contradictory elements that are identical, in different planes.
3. Tracing the intangible, by studying the opposite values, intangible is reached, clarifying the known and unknown contra-indicators.
4. An effort transforms mass into energy—effort is the force when applied satisfies Newton's Second Law of Motion.
5. Creative and Action Process—Proof of Knowledge: Modern physics has thus revealed that every subatomic particle not only performs an energy dance but also is an energy dance, a pulsating process of creation and destruction.
6. Intangible is defined.
7. Spreadsheet Organization Structure: A static organization, flat and crippled whereas Governance is dynamic and never static. A great mismatch.
8. The Implication—matter and energy what ought to be vis-à-vis the governance.

Action Points

1. Measure Intangible
2. Measure dynamic Governance
3. Measure Cost Consequence now, now, now

Notes

1. G. McCool, M. Graybow. 2009. "Madoff Gets 150 Years for Massive Investment Fraud." https://www.reuters.com/article/us-madoff/madoff-gets-150-years-for-massive-investment-fraud-idUSTRE55P6O520090629.
2. Pramanas—Hindu Dharma—Nyaya. http://www.kamakoti.org/hindudharma/part13/chap3.htm.
3. "Arthapatti is a Sanskrit term meaning 'presumption' or 'implication.' Arthapatti refers to the way in which knowledge is derived from a set of circumstances. It is analogous in contemporary logic to the concept of circumstantial implication. It generally requires an observation of fact(s) and postulation based on such fact(s) to arrive at the information." https://www.yogapedia.com/definition/9380/arthapatti.
4. "Anumana is a Sanskrit word that means 'inference' or 'knowledge that follows.'" https://www.yogapedia.com/definition/5901/anumana.
5. "Linga is a Sanskrit word meaning a 'form' or 'symbol.'" https://www.yogapedia.com/definition/5310/linga.
6. J.R. Iyer. 2012. "Who Is the Inside Trader—Rajat Gupta, Rajaratnam, Goldman Sachs or Warren Buffett?" http://bit.ly/2qxAJEs.
7. OECD. "Mr. Joseph E. Murphy (Corporate Compliance and Ethics Professional)." In: *Review of the OECD Anti-bribery Instruments: Compilation of Responses to Consultation Paper*, March 31, 2008.

CHAPTER 5

Measuring the Intangible

Pray as though everything depended on God. Work as though everything depended on you.

—Saint Augustine*

Let us move to recognizing, identifying, and measuring the intangible during the creation of Substance and its follow-up Action Process.

Anything you can connect to, all experiments, take place in the tangible domain. The domain of the intangible does not "exist," in the real sense of the word, because "existence" itself is part of the tangible domain. Seeking to connect to the intangible while in the tangible domain is an experiment akin to antimatter being chased by the scientists in the physical world. Yet, experiments by scientists at NASA and CERN are essential to unravel the mystery of space. It is equally essential in the mundane field to identify the area of influence of the intangible, for the betterment of governance.

The Creation of Substance

A Substance has the inherent characteristics of Quality and Action, which cannot be separated from it. The work is always associated with it, like a piece of cloth and the threads constituting it. Substance combines with Quality and with Activity. When one Substance combines with another Substance, they are yoked together but remain independent. Like a "government by the people, of the people, for the people," each one is a Substance with the same Quality but differentiated by the activity. The purpose is to create a Substance first.

A Substance is the result of a series of transformations from subtle to gross, from concept to being. The lesser the number of qualities, the

---

*https://www.catholic.com/magazine/online-edition/st-ignatius-said-what

subtler it is. Looking at the "government by the people, of the people, and for the people" one can observe Substance with a single quality running through its veins—"governance." There is symmetry in nature, where governance is universal, all-pervasive, and yet subtlest of all. Effort at its subtlest level is conceptual, an idea that needs to be transformed into a Substance to make it worthwhile for a dynamic action of energy to flow.

Distinctly there are two independent processes that takes place.

Creative Process

In this, government by the people is subtler than the subtle. Its meaning needs to be examined, discussed, debated, and defined through sections, clauses, and sub-clauses. It means a policy is created. That is the Creative Process. It ends with a Plan of Action. That Plan is a Substance. For example, UNCAC as a policy document was the outcome of a Creative Process. This Substance, like many such plans, is critical for Action to follow. For action there must be a Substance. This is the most significant aspect of corporate managers' understanding of Substance. Companies, for example, declare themselves signatories to the UNGC. The UNGC has 10 principles under four issue areas and is a Substance of Quality. It is no different from machinery or building, except that one is intangible whereas the other is tangible. Merely being a signatory means little unless they have proven action undertaken by way of certification. An IPR is a substance and can be accommodated in the balance sheet, once the IPR is patented. To accommodate a brand value or UNCAC or HACCP, we shall measure such qualitative elements in the intangible way. With the aid of intangible as a constant, when quantitative elements go by the first stage of senses, qualitative elements have to go by the third stage of intuitive knowledge and be made measurable. By expanding the balance sheet with Quality, Substance expands corporate capability.

Action Process

Substance is the end product of the Creative Process when the Action Process begins. The Substance is created in a linear expansion from nothing.

MEASURING THE INTANGIBLE   69

Strategy Plan is a Substance of Quality, which also takes shape step by step from nothing.

At each stage of the Creative Process, qualitative change takes place from the subtle to the gross level. This gradual progression connects the critical control points of measurement, culminating in a gross object or mental state. The sequence of progression of the Effort can be learned from nature in the way its Quality is personified for governance.

The Corporate Transformation Cause

Substance is created in six steps, as illustrated in Figure 5.1.

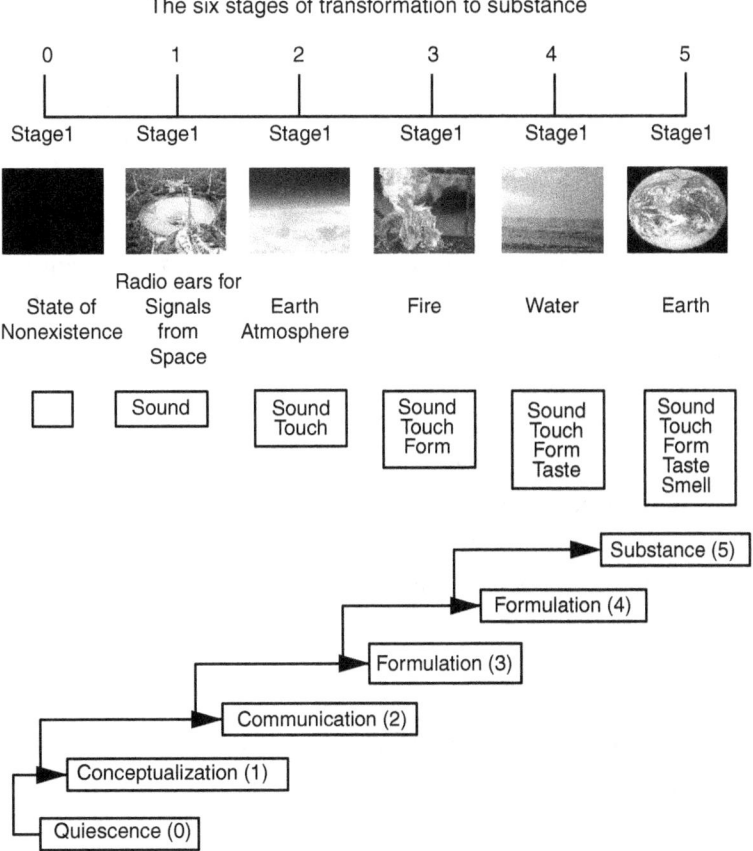

Figure 5.1 The six stages of transformation to substance

There are three layers: (1) nature, (2) sync corporate strategy, and (3) process development.

1. (a) State of quiescence: The six stages of development are evident. They start from the domain of the intangible to create substance in the tangible domain. The first state is the state of quiescence. This is a state of nonexistence. In the beginning, it is a deep mental state before the Big Bang. No quality is attributed to this state, ergo, it is a state of nonexistence.

1. (b) Corporate: Dhirubhai Ambani, founder of Reliance Industries, India, was a great visionary. His vision statement is succinct, consists of four issue areas, and relates to the strategic planning stages of process development. The first part of the statement is, "Our dreams have to be bigger." Anyone's vision starts at this phase, in the domain of the intangible. It is the same for corporate. It is a phase of nonexistence, time to dream big. We see Unilever brands Sunlight detergent or Lux toilet soap in use for nearly a hundred years. The "what's good for General Motors is good for America" syndrome is like a puppy that chases its tail. The power to leave where you are stuck now or choose how you want to move forward in 100 years, even if that means dropping a couple of brands, is possible to contemplate in this state of quiescence. You may apply the same to any major brand, be it Microsoft, Apple, or Tesla. It is repetitive no doubt but protective, under the canopy of corporate. In the future, IPRs may be owned by only individuals, and corporate may need to revisit its strategies. Marc Benioff says that "capitalism, as we know it, is dead." A pole-shift theory of capitalism, with spontaneous optimism, would do the trick in this phase of quiescence.

1. (c) Rating: Process Development Stage 1—State of Quiescence—Ranking 0. The power of 0, where a tangible element is not seen.

2. (a) Space: This is the second phase of the six transformation points. The subtlest of the elements created is space. It has only one quality element—sound.

> There's an interesting scientific discovery on this score, a message from beyond the stars. NASA's Voyager 1 spacecraft sent its first transmission after leaving the earth's solar system. This is the incredible sound recording beamed back to Earth from Voyager 1 as it crossed a new frontier, becoming the first spacecraft ever to leave

the solar system. The rising tones NASA observed are made by the vibration of dense plasma or ionized gas and were captured by the probe's plasma wave instrument. Speaking in a news conference, Don Gurnett, principal investigator for the Voyager plasma wave investigation, said: When you hear this recording, please recognize that this is a historic event. It's the first time that we've ever made a recording of sounds in interstellar space.[1]

It is a proof of concept, scientifically established that the first element sound is from space. Science proved it for the first time but it was mentioned centuries before in India that of the *pancha bhuta*, the five elements, space had only one, sound.

2. (b) Corporate: The strategy that "Our dreams have to be bigger" rings a bell to the visionary. It is the sound that takes the visionary from the domain of the intangible to the reality of the tangible domain, from a dream state to a waking state. Mahatma Gandhi was sitting alone on the parapet wall of the Sabarmati River when he had a brain wave. He decided to start a salt satyagraha the next day, a long march toward the seashores of Dandi, a village in Gujarat. At the seashore, on April 6, 1930, with a lump of salt in his hand, he declared, "With this, I am shaking the foundations of the British empire," and he did. In the same manner, dreaming big can shake the foundations of the corporate world. This is the phase of thought and ideas.

Corporate is governed by the most active senses. While reflecting in Stage 1, in the intangible domain, a break from reason is called for. Carlos Castaneda, author of *The Teachings of Don Juan: A Yaqui Way of Knowledge*, says fear is the first natural enemy a man must overcome on his path to knowledge. Freedom of enterprise is stunted by a fear of everything, fear of the known and more the fear of the unknown. What is significant is that the Strategy Idea may begin in Stage 2, which is at the lowest stage of senses at work, with a single element in-store but is yet to be developed further. Several fault lines in capitalism need a good shake from the past, to cause a revolution now that will set a course of action for the future.

2. (c) Rating: Process Development Stage 2—It rings a bell—a sound—an idea—Conceptual stage: Ranking 1, reflecting a single element.

3. (a) Air, which is less pervasive, in addition to sound, has the quality of touch that can be heard and felt.

3. (b) Corporate: Strategy Planning has begun setting its ambitions higher, by communicating the Strategy Idea. There are three stages by which Strategy Planning takes place. This stage is the first one. A conceptual idea needs to be communicated. This not only leads to a brainstorming session but primarily serves the function of communicating the idea to a select few to test its validity. It's a crucial aspect of business transformation—convincing others of your ideas. Those who are chasing NPAs or promoting a cheat software tend to skip this aspect, and it is the lead cause for subsequent disaster. Despite the process of communication, if you are yet chasing NPAs or heavy penalties, you need to change up your close confidants. They may have failed you, but it is also time to question yourself, as to whether your ideas are worth their salt. Don't get stuck to some brands because it had once been too good to you. Setting your ambitions higher is at a matured stage after strenuous intellectual effort.

3. (c) Rating: Process Development Stage 3—Communication stage: Ranking 2, reflecting two elements.

4. (a) Fire has three quality elements, in addition to sound and touch, it possesses a form that can be heard, felt, and seen.

4. (b) Corporate: Strategy Planning steps up by forming a team for the execution of strategy ideas after clearance from the select members of the strategy group. Ambitions are not merely quantitative goals but qualitative ones and a necessary means to move forward. Team members translate the strategy idea into a Strategic Plan.

The Tamil classic text the *Thirukkural* by the poet Thiruvalluvar consists of 1,330 couplets in three parts—virtue, wealth, and love. Verse #517 states, "After having considered, 'this man can accomplish this, from these means,' let (the king) leave with him the discharge of that duty." Corporate speaks often of the delegation of authority but fails at practicing it well. Forming a team is an opportunity for the delegation of authority to trickle down to the foot soldier. The several fault lines we see within corporate all stem from the lack of governance. Hence, this clause has the goal of achieving self-governance, the issue area that is a dominant aspect of management. A foot soldier is free to determine his or her performance through self-governance. There are two aspects to its successful implementation: (i) intellectual capability and (ii) reverse mentoring. Reverse mentoring establishes the foot soldier as an important aspect of management, as all above listen and work toward self-governance. The role of a supervisor is thus reversed, and inverts who listens and who is listened to, in the hierarchy of corporate management. Risk culture, therefore, spreads to the lowest-ranking person as well as to each above. The LIBOR fiasco mentioned earlier arose since risk appetite is top-down disastrous management that doesn't spread risk culture. Team formation for the relative Strategy Idea is crucial to set the tone for the next 100 years, as to the qualitative elements of management. The fault lines one finds of the past are all qualitative and therefore selection of team members would be critical for the Strategy Idea to be converted to set goals and targets at this formation stage.

4. (c) Rating: Process Development Stage 4—Formation stage: Ranking 3, reflecting three elements.

5. (a) Water has four quality elements—sound, touch, form, and taste. It can be heard, touched, seen, and tasted. The unique element present in water is taste and consequently discrimination.

5. (b) Corporate: The stage is set for formulating policies and setting targets, to construct values and deconstruct the valueless that have been the stumbling block of corporate growth in the past. The purpose is to come out with a Strategy Plan, a comprehensive statement of projections that reflect the Strategic Idea formulated in Stage 1. An idea well-conceived in Stage 1, from the domain of the intangible, is carried through Formulation Stage 5, in the tangible domain, toward a thoroughly developed substance in varying degrees of perfection. The prime factor in Keynes's Animal Spirits is the spontaneous urge to action rather than inaction. In reality, managers get stuck at this stage, because they are mired in chasing quantitative benefits multiplied by quantitative probabilities. At the end of it, there is none to bell the cat. It is spontaneous optimism that animal spirits propound. Managers are reluctant to commit themselves for a variety of factors, moral, hedonistic, or economic. Ethical motive supported by many a principled policy that would form part of management quality needs to be written as a set of rules for each policy. A Strategy Plan is a substance of Quality and Action. Hence, how these rules and by whom they would be conducted are being made ready

at this stage. It is a single individual who comes out with a great idea, be it a Steve Jobs or Thomas Watson Jr. or Bill Gates. Invariably, they are successful because of the previous stage, forming the right team. This stage hinders progress for many a company because of the managerial hesitation to commit. This phase comes out with a Strategy Plan, projecting say 7 years into the future, setting ambitions higher, determined by the quality of the plan.

5. (b) Rating: Process Development Stage 5—Formulation Stage: Ranking 4, reflecting four elements.

6. (a) The earth has five qualities: sound, touch, form, taste, and smell, that is, it can be heard, touched, seen, tasted, and smelled. The matter is in the completed form. The transformation cause is wholesome, and the effect is a Substance.

6. (b) Corporate: This stage is the culmination of five stages of intense analysis of past, present, and future, from a single company connected to a global GDP. It is the stage of committing deeper the strategy idea onto a paper. Strategy Plan is a Substance of Quality and Action. Creative Process ends in a Substance of Quality. A Substance can be UNCAC, HACCP, an IPR, Code of Conduct, CoBP, balance sheet, profitability statement, and so on. It is all-pervasive.

6. c. Rating: Process Development Stage 6—Substance Stage: Ranking 5, reflecting five elements (Table 5.1).

At each stage, one element is added to the completion of the previous step. So, there are no decimal ratings. The successive advancement to the next stage is not a work-in-progress but a moving forward to the next stage on completion of the previous one. From Stage 2 onward the movement has clear cut-off points, which are tangible. Corporate gets stuck,

Table 5.1 Ratings for creative process

Stage	Effort	Rating
Stage 1	Nonexistent	0
Stage 2	Conceptualization	1
Stage 3	Communication	2
Stage 4	Formation	3
Stage 5	Formulation	4
Stage 6	Substance	5

as mentioned earlier, in the Stage 5, Formulation Stage, and somehow reaches the last stage of the Creative Process, that is, the emergence of Strategy Plan. Somehow, at the Formulation Stage in the tangible domain means one is not moving toward a thoroughly developed substance in varying degrees of perfection. Quality of the emerging substance is determined by the Formulation Stage 5. The Creative Process follows an identical growth process in all Substances, be it man-made or natural. A baby may take 9 months, a diamond a few years, an IPR a few weeks, a policy a few hours, but the process is chronologically successive, yet separate. There is no quantum jump. As Warren Buffett put it: "No matter how great the talent or efforts, some things just take time. You can't produce a baby in one month by getting nine women pregnant." A Strategy Plan is as detailed as a flight manual, for an Action Process to follow, in order accidents are avoided, to run smoothly. Many an entrepreneur fails when he tries a quantum jump.

Intellectual Value Capital

Creative Process is the Intellectual Value Capital of a company consisting of several independent Substances of Quality and Action Plans. Intellectual Value Capital is measured by a simple addition of each such Substance created, divided by the number of Substances. The resultant figure indicates the completed stage of development and achievement. If any single Substance is below par, the rating would be of the lowest grade. Otherwise, Substance such as UNCAC, COSO Framework adopted, each would get a value of 5, each a substance of Quality and Action Plan. If the Code of Conduct (CoC) is prepared as an Ethical Strategy Plan but valued below par, say 2, Intellectual Value Capital of say two factors UNCAC and CoC will equal 5+2 divided by 2 resulting in the value of Intellectual Value Capital of a company to be 3. Any number of such Substances can be added to arrive at Intellectual Value Capital but in spite of having a Quality document like UNCAC if others do not match in quality, Intellectual Value Capital value comes down. This is evident when UNCAC is 5 but CoC is only 2. All such qualitative policy documents are yoked together but valued independently. It is imperative all policy documents are well structured and by itself each is valued at the optimum of 5, like the UNCAC. We convert raw materials into finished products so as to sell them off—that is the purpose. The same is the case for creating a policy document, such as the UNCAC, or whistleblower policy, to ensure they are strictly followed. These policies have been created from the unknown and brought to a known level as an Object so that Action Process is easy.

Action Process

It is unique to the quality of the respective Creative Process documentation. For example, the results of violation of human rights, labor rights, environmental rights or anti-corruption drive, corporate governance, risk management, profitability statements, CoC, whistleblower policy would look to the respective Quality document to comply with standards or targets. So would an IPR, product innovation for its Quality and Action of the Substance. Each is unique, pin to pin, plane to plane. Action Process starts at a gross level. This follows the same Six Stages of Transformation to Substance. The Creative Process starts at the level of non-existence whereas the Action Process begins at the level of insentience. If, after all the trouble taken to create a CoC document, it has been "read, laughed and filed code," then it is said to be in a state of insentience. It is common in very many countries who were signatories to the UNCAC to start with, and after several years ratify UNCAC but do not create an anti-corruption body or bodies under Article 6, the preventive anti-corruption clause. The implication of not having a head for such a body is quite alarming in the context of the anti-corruption drive, in particular, Article 46, Mutual Legal Assistance, states, "The provisions of this article shall not affect the obligations under any other treaty, bilateral or multilateral, that governs or will govern, in whole or in part, mutual legal assistance." The head of the UNCAC in a country can overrule any other bilateral or multilateral treaty signed and sealed by that country. The head of the UNCAC is so empowered but nevertheless finds himself powerless to operate.

The targets are set in six scales during the Action Process and akin to the Creative Process. It reflects establishing the performance scales in the same manner for both the Creative Process and the Action Process. The ratings of 0 to 5 in the Action Process sync with the Creative Process ratings accordingly. Only one among the many belong to the quantitative element of management—profitability statement and balance sheet—the rest are qualitative. For example, project management or HACCP or UNCAC implementation, Strategy Plan will have a detailed Action Plan with targets set in the Action Process. There is no half-hearted attempt that would be acceptable. Hence, when the ratings in six scales relate to the ratings of the Creative Process, say rated 3, it means it is at the Formation Stage. That is to say, the team is not formed yet, to take corrective action to lift the task accomplishments to an optimum level of performance. Deeply looking at these phenomena of corrective action leads naturally to the Creative Process. This will be taken up in later chapters Table 5.2.

Table 5.2 Ratings for action process

Stage	Effort	Performance (Percent)	Rating
Stage 1	Insentient	<0	0
Stage 2	Conceptualization	>0 <25	1
Stage 3	Communication	>25 <50	2
Stage 4	Formation	>50 <75	3
Stage 5	Formulation	>75 <100	4
Stage 6	Task Accomplishment	>100	5

Properties of the Creative Process and the Action Process

1. The Creative Process is a product of the intangible and Six Stages of Transformation to Substance represented by Quality that must be present to measure the status of a Substance.
2. There are two aspects to Action in Substance: (1) Effort and (2) Performance.
3. In the case of Action Process of Substance, Effort is apparent whereas in the case of Substance of Quality, the Effort leads from conceptual thought.
4. In the case of the Creative Process, the end product is Substance whereas the end product for Action Process is task accomplishment, which can end up creating another Substance when goes for corrective action that needs a rehash of the process. Another Substance is warranted when fault lines during the Action Process are rectified.

5. In the Action Process, when targets are set, Performance and Effort are in various scales of achievement; the process characteristics reflect the manner by which target goals are met, lethargic to active participation of individuals and team members.

Action Value Capital

Action Value Capital is the culmination of tasks accomplished in an infinite succession of finite purposes by controlling each goal. We have the capability to control huge corporate data. Action Process is the triggering device of the mind. Action is the purpose of the creation of Substance. It follows the same principle of the Creative Process. The stages of development are the same. If the Action Process of two Process Blocks is completed, the ranking by Table 5.2 would be the basis. Each quantitative item, like sales, consumption, advertising expenses, would be an independent process block. We shall take up process blocks in detail later. Since Action starts on a gross object, it is quantitative with targets set for tasks accomplished. The six stages are calculated in equal distribution. Some may perform to obtain 3, another 3, and another 5. The average for three different process blocks, say, inventory reduction, sales targets, consumption targets, in this case is $11/3 = 3$, taking only the integer. This would be the same for every Substance acted upon. Action Value Capital is therefore 3. Note combining two different types of process blocks, because we are measuring the Effort put in and the Performance of individuals, related to the stage they have completed.

Intangible Value Capital

Intangible Value Capital is the average sum of Intellectual Value Capital and Action Value Capital, of the Creative Process and the Action Process, respectively. Assuming Intellectual Value Capital is 4, the average sum of several process blocks, and Action Value Capital is the aforementioned 3, then the Intangible Value capital is arrived at as follows:

Intangible Value Capital = [Intellectual Value Capital + Action Value Capital]/2;

That is = $[4 + 3]/2$; = 3

Profitability Statement and Balance Sheet would form part of the Action Value Capital. Value is derived by targets set and performance measured.

The enterprise valuation is 3. Optimum level is 5 by each individual Substance. Index of Inactivity would be [5–3] = 2. The gap needs to be filled by each process area and by each person to reach the optimum level of performance. Further calculation will be explained later with a case study.

Chapter 5: Points to Ponder

1. The creation of substance: Mass and energy have an equivalence: Energy is liberated matter; matter is energy waiting to happen. Every subatomic particle not only performs an energy dance but also is an energy dance, a pulsating process of creation and destruction. The creation of substance is the natural process of corporate planning. What we are hitherto confined to look at as tangible matter that forms only fiscal assets, here we also look into the creation of ethical assets. The Strategy Plan encompasses both ethical assets and fiscal assets. This time emphasis is on ethical assets and how shall they be created to be active and make their subatomic particles dance. The future of corporate, its very existence as a strong, robust organization, would be on this score where energy is from liberated ethical assets.

2. Creative Process analyzed by way of the Six Stages of Transformation to Substance, a step by step chronologically successive advancement toward creating an ethical asset. This provides the basis of measurement of six stages beginning from the domain of the intangible. There are five elements that progress at each stage to facilitate creating a substance of quality and action integrated. The long-awaited scientific proof for sound as the only element from space reaffirms the age-old theory of *pancha bhuta*—the five elements that constitute creating a substance.

3. Properties of the Creative Process and the Action Process are highlighted: The Creative Process is termed as the Intellectual Value Capital for corporate and the Action Process the Action Value Capital. Together, Intangible Value Capital for corporate will be the main criterion for measurement of the Intangible.

4. Addresses the issue raised earlier, measuring the intangible, measure dynamic Governance—at each stage then and there—and

measure Cost Consequence now, now, now—by an Index of Inactivity, which will be taken up further in the remaining chapters.

Action Points

1. Prepare Corporate: Intangible Value Capital.
2. Create Corporate Index of Inactivity, a matrix by Process Area and by Resource Area, where Process Area represents corporate functions and Resource Area represent the one and the only resource corporate has—pulsating energy—the intangible.

Note

1. Associated Press. 2013. "A Message from beyond the Stars: NASA's Voyager 1 Spacecraft Sends First Transmission after Leaving Earth's Solar System." https://www.dailymail.co.uk/sciencetech/article-2420739/First-sound-recording-solar-beamed-Earth-NASA-Voyager-1-spacecraft.html#ixzz57BBIs2Sl.

CHAPTER 6

Inactivity Based Cost Management

An Activity has a cost incidence whereas Inactivity a cost consequence. Measure Cost Consequence, Now, Now, Now.

—Jayaraman Rajah Iyer*

Inactivity Based Cost Management[1] (IBCM) functions on the following five principles:

1. Principle #1: What gets measured, gets managed
2. Principle #2: Measure Qualitative Elements of Management
3. Principle #3: Corporate Atomic Structure
4. Principle #4: Return on Intangible
5. Principle #5: Emergent Property Phenomenon

Principle #1: What Gets Measured, Gets Managed

Some of the notable events in corporate history provide evidence of this. Lockheed, an American aerospace company, was the first major financial scandal that rocked the corporate world, in 1976. Then secretary of state Henry Kissinger maintained that disclosure would harm other governments and damage U.S. relations with them.[2] There was one minor consolation: Reports of rampant payoffs by Exxon, Gulf, Mobil, Northrop, United Brands, and other corporate giants had not directly implicated any major world leaders.[3] Ashland Oil Inc. argued that securities laws did not require public disclosure of the recipients of questionable payments the company claimed to have made in Nigeria, Gabon, Libya, and

---

*Inactivity Based Cost Management

the Dominican Republic. Ashland had already supplied the names to the SEC. Lockheed went further. It stated that identifying its beneficiaries could hurt its $1.6 billion backlog of unfilled foreign orders, presumably by causing embarrassed foreign governments to cancel contracts, and also damage prospects for future sales. Nor would Lockheed promise to make no more political payments. Such payments, it said, are a normal and necessary feature of doing business in certain parts of the world, are essential to sales, and "are consistent with practices engaged in by numerous other companies abroad."[4]

A report from the Reserve Bank of Australia Bulletin February 1995[5] analyses the collapse of Barings Bank, thanks to the reckless actions of Nick Leeson. The Board of Banking Supervision concluded that the failings at Barings could not be attributed to the complexity of the business carried out within BFS (Baring Futures [Singapore]) but were primarily a failure on the part of a number of individuals within the Barings Group to do their jobs properly. Against that background, the board outlined five main lessons for management flowing from the Barings failure:

1. Management teams have a duty to understand fully the businesses they manage.
2. Responsibility for each business activity has to be clearly established and communicated to all relevant parties.
3. Clear segregation of duties is fundamental to any effective control system.
4. Relevant internal controls, including independent risk management, have to be established for all business activities.
5. Top management and the audit committee have to ensure that significant weaknesses, identified to them by internal audit or otherwise, are resolved quickly.

What emerges from these findings is that there's no measurement system for ethical behavior within these companies. That concept is completely missing. The range of such wrongdoings has only increased from 1976 to 1995 to 2019. This period has witnessed the downfall of firms such as Enron, Robert Maxwell, Madoff, IL&FS, and the slow but sure diminishing of the Big 8 audit firms to the Big 4 firms. Referring to the audit committee seems to be the standard panacea for such ongoing corporate ills. A common streak is that these downfalls have each been caused by the actions of a single individual freely running amok with a license of hedonism akin to that in the 007 James Bond movie *Goldfinger*. Charles Ferguson's *Inside Job* reveals a lot about these perpetrators. Some of the interviewees have described the lavish lifestyle of Richard Fuld, CEO of Lehman Brothers, replete with mansions, private elevators, an art collection filled with million-dollar paintings, a bunch of corporate planes. Jeffrey Lane, vice chairman of Lehman Brothers (2003–2007), says, "Fifty-billion-dollar deals were not large enough, so we do hundred billion-dollar deals." Willem Buiter, chief economist of Citigroup, says, "Banking became a pissing contest, you know; mine's bigger than yours; that kind of stuff. It was all men that ran it, incidentally." It is also worthy of note that none of the errant bosses in each of these scandals were women. The intangible, a force that converts mass into energy and vice versa, does not have a gender bias. In fact, when applying the measure to management, it is more likely that women will reach board-level appointments by their sheer performance on intangible measurements than men.

Illustratively, in the Government Auditing Standards January 2007 Revision issued by the U.S. Government Accountability Office,[6] the word "governance" has been used 60 times and barring two, it is prefixed with the phrase "those charged with." It implies (1) governance is a staff function and there are individuals who are not entrusted with governance and (2) audits are undertaken in the same pattern as balance sheet audit. "Performance audit objectives may vary widely and include assessments of program effectiveness, economy, and efficiency; internal control; compliance; and prospective analyses."[7] In both the cases understanding of governance needs further explanation. The expression "those charged with governance" is akin to "those who are charged with breathing."

The simple fact is what gets measured, gets managed. This is the first resolution an organization should believe in, for other benefits to follow. Governance needs to be measured, only then can governance be managed.

Principle #2: Measure Qualitative Elements of Management

A global survey of 378 senior executives, jointly conducted by KPMG International with the Economist Intelligent Unit (EIU), on corporate sustainability, concluded,

> Many firms are grappling with the problem of deciding exactly what and how to measure, and appropriate benchmarks are scarce. Deciding how to measure is more difficult than deciding what to measure with 78% of respondents considering creating or finding reliable internal data, 76% finding a meaningful benchmark, and 65% determining what to report on, a "major" or "moderate" challenge.[8]

Corporate needs to scrutinize their buzzwords carefully. "Sustainability" is another such that remains unexamined. A way to bypass this is to first apply the #1 Principle test, that is, what gets measured, gets managed. In the KPMG–EIU survey, the respondent base was highly placed: 26 percent were CEOs, presidents, or managing directors of their firms; half represented the C-suite or board, and all respondents were in a management position. Measuring qualitative elements of management will have to be addressed squarely.

Principle #3: Corporate Atomic Structure (Figure 6.1)

Restructure the Organization

The intangible is the energy force that pervades corporate. In the Subject–Object distinction between the Qualitative and Quantitative elements of corporate management, the Subject, a person possessing the pulsating energy, delves into matters of metaphysics. The Object is inert, but its logical structure is unique with Quality and Action integrated. The Subject is the driver of movement in man-made Objects. By the second principle, we found many corporate managers knew what to measure but struggled with how to measure. What Galileo said could be meaningful: "Measure what is measurable, and make measurable what is not so." Organizational restructuring is called for to accommodate issue areas we find difficult to measure.

INACTIVITY BASED COST MANAGEMENT 85

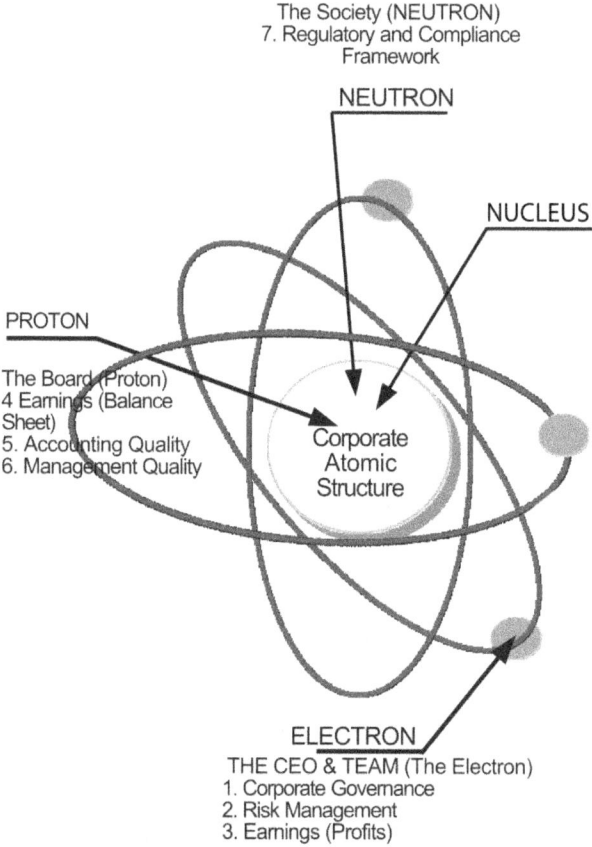

Figure 6.1 3-D corporate atomic structure

Redesign with a 3-D Corporate Atomic Structure

Corporate needs to discard the 2-D spreadsheet organization structure currently in use. When the intangible is placed in the pivotal position, the organization structure revolves around it. The intangible is a metaphysical concept. The Kantian ideal of the science of metaphysics with a logical structure like that of the well-established mathematical and natural sciences is now made possible. A 3-D Corporate Atomic Structure reflects the natural formation of atomic structure, with only two processes in the making. By connecting the laws of physics to metaphysics, lasting metrics, measures of quantitative assessment, are established. Martin Rees, a British cosmologist and astrophysicist, talking about aliens says, though they may come from planet Zog and have seven tentacles, they would be made of similar atoms to us. That's not an issue here, for corporate has not thought about

Table 6.1 Similarity between atomic structure and corporate atomic structure

Atomic structure	Corporate atomic structure
1. Every atom is made from three kinds of elementary particles: protons, which have a positive electrical charge; electrons, which have a negative electrical charge; and neutrons, which have no charge.	1. Every substance is made up of three kinds of elementary particles: policies, which have a positive charge; practices, which have a negative charge; and the society, which has no charge.
2. Protons and neutrons are packed into the nucleus, while electrons spin around outside.	2. Policies and the society are packed into the nucleus, while practices spin around outside.
3. The number of protons in an atom is always balanced by an equal number of electrons.	3. The number of categories of personnel in policies is always balanced by an equal number of categories in practices.
4. Neutrons don't influence an atom's identity, but they do add to its mass.	4. Society doesn't influence the identity of a company, but it does add to its mass.
5. ($e = mc^2$): e in the equation stands for energy, m for mass, and c square for the speed of light squared.	
In the simplest term, what the equation says is that mass and energy have an equivalence. They are two forms of the same thing: Energy is liberated matter; matter is energy, waiting to happen.	
Since c^2 (speed of light by itself) is a truly enormous number, what the equation is saying is that there is a huge amount, a REALLY huge amount, of energy bound up in every material thing.	

being one with nature. They stand aloof from the laws of physics; rather corporate structure as of now is alien to the entire universe, indeed. First of all, let corporate gather momentum to sync with physics, by creating a Corporate Atomic Structure. Let us compare the similarities between the Atomic Structure and Corporate Atomic Structure (Table 6.1):

What Corporate Atomic Structure Means

Every Substance is made up of three kinds of elementary particles: policies, which have a positive charge; practices, which have a negative charge; and society, which has no charge.

1. The most significant part of a 3-D Corporate Atomic Structure is that society is brought into the structure. This means it is integrated into the Corporate Management Operating System. The impact on the Corporate Value System would be immense.

i) Policies are the protons of an organization, from the date of incorporation. Headed by a board of directors, policies set the corporate goals.

ii) Practices are the electrons of an organization, headed by the CEO team.

iii) Society is the neutron of an organization.

2. Policies and society are packed into the nucleus, while practices spin around outside.

   i) The day the registrar of companies approves, a company is dragged into society, with all the paraphernalia of regulators joining in.

   ii) The board and society form a nucleus.

   iii) In the Atomic Structure, protons and neutrons form a nucleus. Protons are 1,837 times the mass of an electron. Electrons spin pretty fast, nearly three-fourth of the speed of light. So fast that they can go off tangent. It's the neutrons that stabilize the electron from spinning off the nucleus.

   iv) In the Corporate Atomic Structure it's society that prevents the CEO from spinning off its nucleus. It greatly stabilizes the functioning of a company.

3. The number of categories of personnel in policies is always balanced by an equal number of categories in practices.

   i) In the Subject–Object Distinction of Qualitative and Quantitative Elements of Management, in the CREAM Report Framework Refer Figure 6.2, the number of people for each task as a team is five, one from the Corporate Ethical Responsibility Force and four from the Corporate Fiscal Responsibility Force. It is irrespective of, for policies or practices that may be under scrutiny of any Process Block.

4. Society doesn't influence the identity of a company, but it does add to its mass.

   i) The neutrons of an organization impact its stability factor. The Ethical Motive triggers the Profit Motive, not the other way around.

5. ($e = mc^2$): e in the equation stands for energy, m for mass, and c^2 for the speed of light squared.

   i) Profits are the energy created by a company. We normally calculate only the fiscal assets, which constitute the mass. Profits are the result of using fiscal assets to the optimum.

ii) Energy is created mainly from ethical assets. What we call c^2 is that it refers to the ethical asset usage. A team of five for each task is backed by an undertaking on ethical responsibility to optimize results.

iii) Sustainability of efficiency, which arises from the best use of fiscal assets, results in profits. Sustainability of Value System, which arises from the best use of ethical assets, adds energy and therefore greater results.

iv) Corporate lives in Plato's cave must go out and find out how ethical standards are practiced and measured, which is not happening, so as to maintain the sustainability of profits and growth.
In the simplest term, what the equation says is that mass and energy have an equivalence. They are two forms of the same thing: Energy is liberated matter; matter is energy, waiting to happen.

v) Cost of Inaction is wasted energy and time, where mass is waiting to be used.

vi) In reality, an electron cannot be stopped as it continuously spins around the nucleus at an unimaginable speed.

vii) Neither should the CEO team, who should never allow fiscal and ethical assets to fall into a state of insentience.

6. Since c^2 (speed of light by itself), is a truly enormous number, what the equation is saying is that there is a huge amount, a really huge amount, of energy bound up in every material thing.

i) That optimum is very huge, represented by c^2. It refers to the Subject; the capability of each individual is truly huge to create a prodigious amount of energy for an organization.

ii) If so, then the profits for a company are indeed huge. Speed of light times the speed of light.

iii) Energy is bound up in every material thing. Release it for the good of society. An organized approach is what is needed for corporate.

007 Factor—The Corporate Benchmark

For corporate to exist as they should requires Corporate Hydrogen, made up of fiscal and ethical assets, be governed in a way that converts mass into energy at the optimized level of performance. Corporate does not do anything more than the universe does: Creative Process and Action

Process, creation and destruction. Nothing else, kicking matter from one space to another. Newton's First Law of Motion applies here: "An object will remain at rest or in uniform motion in a straight line unless acted upon by an external force." We may add two steps to it: First, recognize the creation of ethical assets as matter or substance, and second, kick the matter thus created to send it from one plane to the other. This process takes place as routinely as operating a piece of machinery. Machinery produces a product and an ethical asset produces energy. The 007 factor will be the corporate benchmark applied to both Fiscal and Ethical Assets. Rees defines the composition of the universe. When we apply the same attributes to corporate, the results would be similar. It creates a "Goldilocks effect" for corporate (Table 6.2).

Table 6.2 Benchmarking corporate atomic structure aligning with atomic structure

Atomic Structure*	Corporate Atomic Structure
1. For the universe to exist as it does requires that hydrogen be converted into helium in a precise but comparatively stately manner, specifically, in a way that converts seven one-thousandths [.007] of its mass into energy.	1. For the corporate to exist as they should, requires Corporate Hydrogen, made up of fiscal and ethical assets, be governed in a way that converts mass into energy at the optimized level of performance and use.
2. Lower that value very slightly, from seven one-thousandths [.007] to six one-thousandths [.006], say, and no transformation could take place: The universe would consist of hydrogen and nothing else.	2. Lower the level of performance and use, even slightly, and no transformation takes place—the company would consist of nonmoving Ethical and Fiscal assets and nothing else.
3. Raise the value very slightly, to eight one-thousandths, and bonding would be so wildly prolific that the hydrogen would long since have been exhausted.	3. Raise the value of use, rather misuse, of any one of the assets, such as diversion of funds, assets base would long since have been exhausted.
4. At .007 state, gravity is perfectly pitched—"critical density" is the cosmologists' term for it—and will hold the universe together at the just-right dimensions to allow things to go on indefinitely. Cosmologists, in their lighter moments, sometimes calls this the "Goldilocks effect"—that everything is just right.	4. At 007 factor of governance, gravity is perfectly pitched between the board of directors, the CEO team, and society, such that it will hold a company together at the just-right dimensions to allow things to go on indefinitely. This would be the "Goldilocks Effect" of Corporate Governance, where everything is Just Right.

*Martin Rees.

Principle #4: Return on Intangible

Return on Intangible shall be seen in the background of what American neuroscientist David Eagleman says,

> If we take a cubic centimeter of one's brain tissue, there are as many connections between them[9] as there are stars in the milky ways in the galaxy. These strange alien landscapes of neurons and synapses, somehow with strange materials, map on to decision making.

The cubic centimeter of each brain, not of a team or a group of elite people who run an organization, but of every human we come across on this planet. Return on intangible is an equation when applied to corporate affairs will have a significant impact on the growth and reaching targets, for it encompasses the capability of every individual with an organization. Truly, return on intangible is a capability model. The equation is as follows:

Return on Intangible = (Action or Inaction)/Intangible.

Action or Inaction in the numerator and Intangible the denominator.

Action is 1 and Inaction is 0. Intangible is always 1, for Intangible reveals human capability that is common to all.

This is the same formula as Newton's Second Law of Motion: Force = mass x acceleration.

The purpose of what the Second Law states is not to keep the mass static, but to keep it moving. That's what a CEO team does, not allowing any substance to rest in a static position. In the Six Stages of Transformation during the Creative Process, there's a continuous movement of linear growth toward creating a substance. In the Action Process, the same Six Stages are replicated toward task accomplishment. In the case of an electron in an atom, there's a continuous movement spinning around the nucleus. It's not so in the case of the corporate electron—the CEO team. So, we have conveniently divided the entire Action Process into six sections. When targets are met the numerator is 1. That is to say, 100 percent task accomplishment gets Action rating to 1, which ensures the mass is moved out and the energy is created.

There's a possibility some may or may not reach their targets. Accordingly, the stage for each task would indicate two factors: (1) stage completed and (2) simultaneous gap between the target and the stage completed. In an organization, there are millions of such tasks assigned to every individual that would be identified as to dT/dT, series of tasks in respective series of Time. This holds good both in the Creative Process and the Action Process. The Creative Process has six stages of development from the domain of the intangible through to a substance in the tangible field. IPR is one such tangible substance. The unavoidable six stages of the Creative Process vary, moving from one phase to another linearly. There is no quantum jump in the Creative Process. These six stages of transformation in the creative process will be useful by setting targets for innovation to quicken or broaden each phase accordingly. Illustratively, in the recent outbreak of COVID-19, The Economist in its 6th May 2020 edition states: More than 7,000 papers on the pandemic - covering everything from virology to epidemiology - have appeared in the past three months. A fifth of them has come out in the past week alone.[12] Innovation is individual-centric and therefore participants in the six stages are made accountable. This book is emphatic about the six stages being completed, stage by stage, lest'the end product ends up lacking quality and accountability. Since the denominator is 1 and the binary value makes it clear as to the stage reached, a corporate rating of active elements and simultaneously of inactive elements is obtained. Return on intangible, therefore, for a company as a whole is a single-digit figure between 0 and 5. When it is below 5 an Index of Inactivity furnishes by process area as well as by resource area, only resource is intangible.

Traditional return on investment (RoI) is replaced by return on intangible (RoI). It triggers the capability of every individual and tracks it.

CREAM Analytics Framework (Figure 6.2)

CREAM stands for the following:

1. C—Corporate Governance
2. R—Risk Management,
3. E—Earnings: split into (i) P&L and (ii) Balance Sheet
4. A—Accounting Quality
5. M—Management Quality

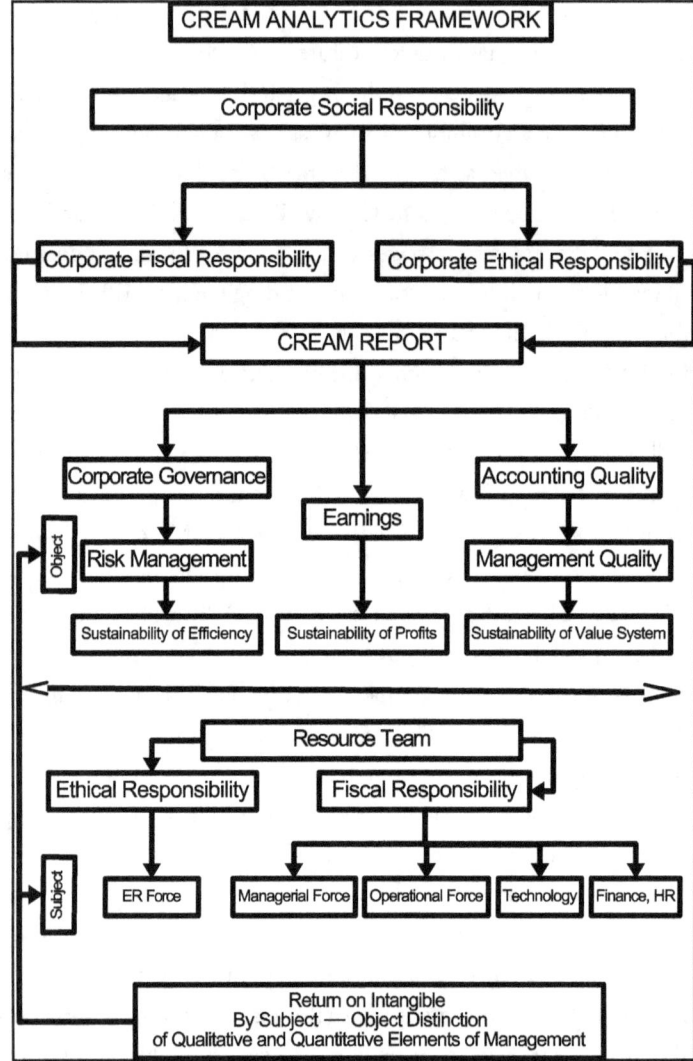

Figure 6.2 CREAM analytics framework

Process Block

Each Process Block has a team of five representing the Ethical and Fiscal Responsibility group. Create Process Blocks for the organization. There are about 170 Process Blocks, as the case study of HUL in Chapter 8 shows—CREAM Report. These open-ended Process Blocks consist of both Qualitative and Quantitative elements of management. Each is manned by a team of five members, one Ethical Responsibility and Four of Fiscal Responsibility.

These Process Blocks come under two categories: Creative Process and Action Process. Nothing more. Each Process Block would fit into either of the two categories. Process Blocks are governed by the CREAM Framework.

Team Formation

It is essential to establish resource owners who would be taking responsibility for all actions of corporate. The resource owners who are classified for the purpose of governance standards are grouped as under:

(1) One Member from the Ethical Responsibility (ER) Group and (2) Four Members from the Fiscal Responsibility Group, consisting of (i) Operational Force, (ii) Managerial Force, (iii) Finance, HR, and other service providers, and (iv) Technology.

ER Force is shown separately, as Governance is for all and Ethical Responsibility is for all. Fiscal Responsibility aligns with Ethical Responsibility.

At a more matured state of Governance, there would be no need to have an ER Force, or for that matter, an Internal Audit Force, separately, as each Process Block is managed by four persons independently well trained in the art of converting their Fiscal and Ethical Assets into pure energy. Each performance is tracked and monitored by return on intangible. Self- Governance must be the ultimate goal of Corporate Ethics. Each task is owned by its team, is entrusted with targets of CAGR converted into CDGR, Daily growth rate. Also, CARR converted into CDRR Daily Reduction Rate, deconstructing what is valueless. Leadership is at the level of organizing the workforce that is entrusted with responsibility, both in the Creative and Action Processes.

The hierarchical one-man call center is no more.

There's no VIP boss anymore, only a foot soldier. In a maintenance team, a cleaner is the foot soldier, in an airplane a pilot is the foot soldier, in a nuclear reactor a doctorate is the foot soldier, in a research lab an innovator is the foot soldier. A hierarchical one-man call center is the bane of corporate development. Risk appetite trickles down from the top. Risk culture travels up from the foot soldier. Remove the distinctions of money from the highest to the lowest paid and compare all as equal. Now, a lowly paid individual can challenge the highest paid on the use of the ethical assets of a company. All have the same cubic centimeter of brain tissue capability, which must be measured and enhanced. That's the principle behind return on intangible. A foot soldier is the surgeon in the operating theatre, and all others readily give the worker what is needed to obtain the desired optimum results. While operating a machine or selling a product, the foot soldier cannot look around in search of a tool, essential for his or her task accomplishment. Remember the adage set by Robert Townsend in *Up the Organization*—"True leadership must be for the benefit of the followers, not the enrichment of the leaders. In combat, officers eat last." The five members in a team during the Action Process are organized to provide that support. If a worker or a salesperson does get the optimum score of five, as well as each person at each step above, there ends the company's woes. CEO rating is arrived at by accumulated ratings of each employee. That is to say, the CEO is concerned about the best ratings of each employee and works toward optimum performance. Intangible is the energy force, and as Polman says, "Leadership is not about giving energy, but unleashing others' people energy"—that fits well with the return on intangible formula. In return on intangible the denominator is the energy force. The optimum score for each person is five. An index of inactivity for the company as a whole identifies a single task by a single person who has not achieved the optimum level of performance. It means the energy force is lacking, which causes the governance deficit, enabling the CEO to take corrective action instantly

Principle #5: Emergent Property Phenomenon

The three principles of emergent property according to Nobel laureate Murray Gellmann are as follows: (1) conformability of nature to herself, (2) applicability of simplicity, and (3) unreasonable effectiveness. By "Emergent Property" he means you don't add something more to get something more. Rather, shed your inhibitions and focus on using your ethical assets. Emergent Property means it's Corporate Yoga.

1. Conformability of nature to herself: "For Nature is very consonant and conformable to herself," says Isaac Newton.[10,11] With Corporate Atomic Structure, the first principle "conformability of nature to herself" is met.
2. Applicability of simplicity: It is ensured by limiting the entire management process to only two: the Creative Process and the Action Process. The second principle of Emergent Property, the applicability of the criterion of simplicity, is met. There are six stages of development and only two processes, the Creative Process and the Action Process. It's simple enough for school children to learn governance by way of a game such as hopscotch.

    Data explosion: Data retained in various forums, the OECD, The Global Competitiveness Report, Central Bureau of Statistics, GDP Growth comparison, World Bank, IMF, National Expenditure on XYZ, is all a nightmare for absorption and comparison. In this work, data is shrunk to the root level. Entire corporate performance by even a single task, by a single individual, can be exploded but yet does not exceed five, and is made meaningful. One is comparable with another. Corporate Atomic Structure is aligned with every other universal benchmark, with the same optimized results. Furthermore, the return on intangible can be calculated not just for one company but for the entire corporate by process area and by resource area, to produce a single result of 0 to 5, with the ready reckoner for Index of Inactivity for each person connected.
3. Unreasonable effectiveness: In return on intangible, covering the entire gamut of management with a single formula, the unreasonable effectiveness principle is met. Unreasonable effectiveness is the art of resolving a paradox with the least number of mathematical calculations. The simplest one is the Opposite Value Analysis, which can resolve any such mental aberrations. It is a truth serum. Return on intangible is a simple process once CAGR is brought to a CDGR level and allocation of duties to individuals part of a team of five is done. Daily performance with task accomplishments and deriving an Index of Inactivity converts the n-dimensional problems to n-problems of one dimension. That one dimension is the denominator, Intangible.

Consider the Organization as Human.

Six Limbs and Four Auxiliary Limbs of a Corporate Body

Let us attribute to a corporate body, a human form. After all, it is made up of people, not inanimate objects. Corporate Returns on Intangible Intellectual Value Capital, of Creative Process, and Action Value Capital, of Action Process, together make the Intangible Value Capital of a company. This is better understood in human terms rather than clinical inanimate ones. Today, an entity is considered an Object with no human involvement, and quantification loses the necessary insight into what human engagement brings to the table. Return on intangible statement of Active Index taken to Wall Street would reveal how vibrant an organization made and run by people actually is.

Six Limbs of the Corporate Body:

1. Nose is the intangible. It converts mass into pure energy.
2. Mouth is the grammar of the Corporate Atomic Structure.
3. Feet are the measurement through Powerful Metrics.
4. Ear is the dictionary of the learning management system (LMS).
5. Eye is the Long-Range Planning and Short-Range Action—CAGR brought to CDGR—Compound Daily Growth Rate, CARR converted into CDRR Daily Reduction Rate.
6. Hand is the work.

Four Auxiliary Limbs of the Corporate Body:

I. Explication of corporate laws and management quality
II. Science of reasoning—sustainability of efficiency
III. Strategies—sustainability of profits
IV. Ethical responsibility—sustainability of value system

With six limbs and four auxiliary limbs, the corporate body in human form may call for attention from a medical team to attend and optimize energy force in respective limbs for an overall health check, limb by limb.

Chapter 6: Points to Ponder

I IBCM—The Five Principles

1. Principle #1: What gets measured, gets managed
2. Principle #2: Measure qualitative elements of management
3. Principle #3: Corporate atomic structure
4. Principle #4: Return on intangible
5. Principle #5: Emergent property phenomenon

II Corporate in Human Form

1. Six limbs of the corporate body
2. Four auxiliary limbs of the corporate body

Notes

1. J.R. Iyer. *Inactivity Based Cost Management*—Copyright REGN. NO. L-27490/2006 dated December 1, 2006 Govt. of India, Copyrights Office.
2. R. Halloran. 1976. "Japanese Raid Lockheed And Others in Bribe Case." https://www.nytimes.com/1976/02/24/archives/japanese-raid-lockheed-and-others-in-bribe-case-japanese-raid-in.html
3. The Big Payoff: TIME: Monday, February 23, 1976.
4. Lockheed's Defiance: A Right to Bribe? TIME: Monday, August 18, 1975.
5. Reserve Bank of Australia. 1995. "Implications of the Barings Collapse for Bank Supervisors."
6. United States Government Accountability Office. 2007. "By the Comptroller General of the United States," Government Auditing Standards. January 2007 Revision.
7. Ibid., 1.28.
8. KPMG International. "Corporate Sustainability A Progress Report," *kpmg.com*. https://www.sustainabilityexchange.ac.uk/files/corporate-sustainability-a-progress-report_1.pdf.
9. D. Eagleman. 2013. " Brain over Mind?" https://www.youtube.com/watch?v=UWBtT-Gl4vQ.
10. Quote from TED talk by M. Gell-Mann. 2007. "Beauty, Truth....and Physics?" https://www.ted.com/talks/murray_gell_mann_beauty_truth_and_physics#t-872257.
11. Also quote from https://libquotes.com/isaac-newton/quote/lbf0m1n.
12. Scientific research on the coronavirus is being released in a torrent: https://www.economist.com/science-and-technology/2020/05/06/scientific-research-on-the-coronavirus-is-being-released-in-a-torrent

CHAPTER 7

The Board of Directors the Corporate Proton

We hire smart people so they can tell us what to do.
—Steve Jobs*

Protons and neutrons are heavier than electrons. One proton is about 1,837 times more massive than an electron. In the case of the Corporate Atomic Structure, the board of directors holds a powerful control over every decision. Protons and neutrons form a nucleus, so do the board and society. The CEO team spins around the corporate nucleus, much like the solar system around the sun. For the universe to exist as it does, hydrogen requires to be converted into helium in a precise but comparatively stately manner. Specifically, in a way that converts seven one-thousandths [0.007] of its mass to energy. So is the case with corporate hydrogen. Money spent in a perfect manner converts financial assets and ethical assets into energy. Lower that value very slightly, from seven one-thousandths [0.007] to six one-thousandths [0.006], say, and no transformation could take place: The universe would consist of hydrogen and nothing else. So is the case with corporate fiscal assets and ethical assets. Kept in a state of insentience, no profits are made, but would see a rise in NPAs. Raise the value slightly, to eight one-thousandths, and bonding would be so wildly prolific that the hydrogen would long since have been exhausted. So is the case with corporate fiscal and ethical assets. When diverted elsewhere without using them to create energy within, there is nothing to produce and sell. At a 007 state, gravity is perfectly pitched, in "critical density" is the cosmologists' term for it. It will hold the universe together at the

---

*Steve Jobs: His Own Words and Wisdom

just-right dimensions to allow things to go on indefinitely. Cosmologists, in their lighter moments, sometimes call this the "Goldilocks effect," when everything is just right. At a 007 factor of governance, gravity is perfectly pitched, between the board of directors, CEO team, and society, such that it will hold a company together at the just-right dimensions to allow things to go on indefinitely. This would be the "Goldilocks Effect" of Corporate Governance—everything is just right. The responsibility to oversee Corporate Critical Density is with the board of directors. Here are four factors that would ensure Corporate Critical Density.

Sustainability

How long can the earth sustain its current state of pristine beauty? The solar system is bound to sustain for another 4.5 billion years.[1] The 007 factor is at ease, with hydrogen converting into helium in a stately manner. Nature is not in a hurry. It is we who are keen for a quantum jump from where we are to a new world. All our isms over the last 500 years have seen humanity spot jogging to end up at square one. Planet earth has moved on. We are static, not the earth. The fact is, we do not know what we want, which is why refugees are seeking sanctuary the world over. Sustainability is another catchword thrown in, unexamined and not scrutinized. The implication of sustainability objectives is all of the ethical responsibility group and call for creating ethical assets by those who undertake the responsibility to act.

The World Commission on Environment and Development refers to sustainability, under 3. Sustainable Development para. 27, thus[2]:

> Humanity has the ability to make development sustainable to ensure that it meets the needs of the present without compromising the ability of future generations to meet their own needs. The concept of sustainable development does imply limits—not absolute limits but limitations imposed by the present state of technology and social organization on environmental resources and by the ability of the biosphere to absorb the effects of human activities.

Without compromising the ability of future generations is an enigma wrapped in mystery contradicted by the present state of technology.

Artificial Intelligence

KPMG, in a recent report, *Rethinking the Value Chain: A Study on AI, Humanoids and Robots,*[3] affirms that

> artificial intelligence will rapidly revolutionize the business world. This is no time for skepticism, hesitancy or a wait-and-see approach. Success in this disruptive environment requires leaders to quickly grasp the relevant aspects of artificial intelligence. Awareness and a sharp eye for emerging opportunities are essential requirements for the sustainability of any company.[4.]

Many are on the bandwagon. Illustratively, Mark Hurd, CEO Oracle, tweeted, "To gain an advantage in the fierce competition for the next generation of organizational leaders, companies should look to #AI." Not necessarily, because the public and the investor community would be looking for a value system practiced within a company, ensuring leadership is in the right hands. We have seen it before with enterprise resource planning (ERP) software packages covering entire global companies. SAP revenue is directly proportional to the fixed costs of many companies. If SAP has to be profitable, many corporates have to contribute. Return on investment is negligible. For example, if one wants to make any changes or add-on to these cost-prohibitive software packages, one has to go through an intermediary that invariably is a high-priced consulting firm. Clearly, the second principle, the applicability of simplicity in Emergent Property, is lost. The inventory module of IBM1401, with a mere 8k capacity, written in Autocoder, has not changed since 1966. Inventory remains a hurdle to achieve JIT. With unutilized capacity, such high-priced ERP packages become white elephants. On a similar note, AI needs to be scrutinized—for whom and by whom is AI being suggested, in a place like India, where there is a surplus of cheap labor.[5] There's a big market no doubt for AI and robots, or one shall say any technological advancement in agriculture. Illustratively, Indian agriculture was languishing at 2.75 percent CAGR during the last decade (2010–2019),[6] and we can set the target to double in the next. If Indian agricultural yield is way below that of other countries, we have to bridge the gap. Let's take one item of agriculture, peanuts, and examine the utility of technology direction. In peanuts yield, we find China ranks 13 and India 32, way behind many a country in the world. Uzbekistan ranks the highest followed by Israel.[7] India stands second in the hierarchy of agriculture for all countries, per data 2017, at $401.32 billion, whereas China is at $968.63 billion.[8] Indian agriculture would be a trillion-dollar economy by its own right in the next 4 years and agri technology has a major role to play. As the Indian agri structure, with farmer producer organisations (FPOs) and farmer producer companies (FPCs), is poised for a major expansion, Project FISCAL (farmer–industry–society & consolidate agri leadership), initiated by yours truly in Gujarat, would help map the entire agriculture sector. Such a farmer–industry–society collaboration would consolidate agri leadership. A technological revolution with ERP or AI, with a balanced approach, would be put to better use. The current inception is not very high. Not every Indian farmer owns a tractor; many lease one for a day or two. AI could make a difference between where the economy stands now and a trillion-dollar agri economy. With every Indian farmer having an identity, an Aadhar Card (a 12-digit unique identification number issued by the Indian government to every individual resident of India) number would identify and track progress toward 2024. Agriculture is the primary source of livelihood for about 58 percent of India's population, says an Indian Brand Equity Foundation (IBEF) report. That's about 750 million people! AI, when used in the agri sector, will fetch a better return than in the heavily laden fixed cost of corporate. So, focusing on AI or robots in the agri sector makes more sense than in a multinational corporate, in which it only serves to increase their fixed cost. In other words, don't make the same mistake with AI that you did with ERP.

The Board of Directors

The 98 Process Blocks under Management Quality, as given in Table 7.1 Index of Inactivity by Process Area and Table 7.2 Index of Inactivity by Resource Area, in their entirety, constitute the measurement of the board members. Chapter 8 analyzes Tables 7.1 and 7.2 further.

In particular, the board of directors consists of nine issue areas, with one board business consisting of 19 issue areas, detailing the duties the board undertakes. Overall, 27 issue areas are measured as to the current status.

Table 7.1 Index of inactivity by process area

Index of inactivity: By process area: CREAM		2007	2008–2009	2016–2017	2017–2018	2018–2019
C—Corporate governance [19]	Active	300	300	350	350	350
	Inactive	175	175	125	125	125
	IA%	36.84%	36.84%	26.32%	26.32%	26.32%
R—Internal controls and risk management [7]	Active	121	121	121	121	121
	Inactive	54	54	54	54	54
	IA%	30.86%	30.86%	30.86%	30.86%	30.86%
E—Earnings: P&L And Balance Sheet [12]	Active	90	118	122	114	122
	Inactive	210	182	178	186	178
	IA%	70.00%	60.67%	59.33%	62.00%	59.33%
A—Accounting quality [16]	Active	218	146	162	139	150
	Inactive	182	254	213	236	225
	IA%	45.50%	63.50%	56.80%	62.93%	60.00%
M—Management quality [98] [97,19]	Active	1,635	1,635	1,741	1,741	1,741
	Inactive	815	815	709	709	709
	IA%	33.27%	33.27%	28.92%	28.92%	28.92%
CREAM report [152/151]	Active	2,364	2,320	2,496	2,465	2,484
	Inactive	1,436	1,480	1,279	1,310	1,291
	IA%	37.79%	38.95%	33.87%	34.69%	34.19%
Total		3,800	3,800	3,775	3,775	3,775
Net rating		3	3	3	3	3
Stage reached	[Legend: 0—Insentient; 1—Conceptual; 2—Communication; 3—Formation; 4—Formulation; 5—Task Done]					
Tally: Resource area ~ Process area		0.00	0.00	0.00	0.00	0.00

Table 7.2 Index of Inactivity by Resource Area

Index of inactivity: by resource area: CREAM		2007	2008–2009	2016–2017	2017–2018	2018–2019
1. ER Management:	Active	290	290	329	329	329
	Inactive	470	470	426	426	426
	IA%	12.37%	12.37%	11.28%	11.28%	11.28%
2. FR: Managerial Force:	Active	519	508	542	533	539
	Inactive	241	252	213	222	216
	IA%	6.35%	6.64%	5.64%	5.89%	5.73%
3. FR: Operating force	Active	519	508	542	538	539
	Inactive	241	252	213	217	216
	IA%	6.35%	6.64%	5.65%	5.75%	5.73%
4. FR: Technology: Active	Active	519	508	542	533	539
	Inactive	241	252	213	222	216
	IA%	6.35%	6.64%	5.65%	5.89%	5.73%
5. FR: Finance	Active	519	507	542	533	539
	Inactive	241	253	213	222	216
	IA%	6.35%	6.66%	5.65%	5.89%	5.73%
ER + FR: Resource area	Active	2,364	2,320	2,496	2,465	2,484
	Inactive	1,436	1,480	1,279	1,310	1,291
	IA%	37.78%	38.96%	33.87%	34.69%	34.19%
Net rating		3	3	3	3	3
Stage reached		\[Legend: 0—Insentient; 1—Conceptual; 2—Communication; 3—Formation; 4—Formulation; 5—Task Done\]				
Tally: Resource area ~ Process area		0.00	0.00	0.00	0.00	0.00

The #1 is that of Ethical Responsibility and the rest of Fiscal Responsibility. While assessing all these issue areas, undertaking Ethical Responsibility is not evident. All the 98 issue areas of Management Quality assessed belong to the Fiscal Responsibility area. The board does not run an organization daily. It meets once in a month and reviews the operations, appointing committees to oversee the running of the organization. The changes that shall come through the board's assessment would be #1 Ethical Responsibility and #2 reviewing and tracking CDGR of the company's growth vis-à-vis CAGR as per the long-term strategy plan already approved by the board. CREAM Report for the entire organization covering open-ended 170 process blocks would be taken up by the board simultaneously. Ethical Assets would revolutionize the board room. CREAM Report rating is a single-digit number between 0 and 5, and the board members can receive it daily. Any single dip by any single person's performance would bring down the overall rating as a wake-up call for the board to react. For example, had a single person from the Ethical Responsibility Force refused to clear planting the cheat software, while all the four Fiscal Responsibility group members wanted to go ahead, the market that was expecting the introduction of the diesel emission control fittings would have reacted adversely on the same day. The board members instantly get to know the market reaction and the dipping of the company's rating. Vision and action go together. The board needs to change for the better while they do have the power to operate. Delineation of duties between the board and the CEO team vis-à-vis society is very clear. Change the denominator.

Reverse Mentoring

A single cubic centimeter of a single brain is more powerful than trillions of robots. When we introduced plastics, we believed it would save paper and therefore the forests. A few centuries since we believed the earth was flat, we assume we have arrived. We have plunged into industry with a quantum jump, discarding the past and embracing the future, blindly. We are Object-oriented, ignoring the Subject. The earth has a finite number of people, who we have not taken into account for the future. Sustainability reports mention "without compromising the ability of future generations to meet their own needs" but do not define our ability to teach the next generation. The refusal to adopt new strategies, like refusing to listen to

Galileo, is the natural stumbling block for progress. China went further, by instructing youth to destroy schools and books in the name of a cultural revolution in China. China is the hierarchical one-man call center, as is evident from its handling of the COVID-19 pandemic, and they need a revolution to take the country from one phase to the other. The corporate board has designed itself in the same fashion as China, as a one-man call center. The components are there, what is needed is an integration of qualitative and quantitative elements, to breathe life into a business entity in human form. GenNext not waiting to listen to you, not wanting to listen to you, not willing to listen to you, but we have to make ourselves known to GenNext—what and how equipped we are—to teach them. GenNext follow us unhesitatingly; that's why they reflect what we do—not waiting to listen to them, not wanting to listen to them, not willing to listen to them. Reverse mentoring needs to happen. It has been so throughout history, the elders listening to GenNext, without which there would have been no progress at all. *Each person has some amazing capabilities that we ignore as we run to robots for wisdom.* As Carl Sagan says, "Every one of us is, in the cosmic perspective, precious. If a human disagrees with you, let him live. In a hundred billion galaxies, you will not find another."[9] Change the denominator.

Chapter 7: Points to Ponder

1. At 007 factor of governance, gravity is perfectly pitched between the board of directors, CEO team, and society and will hold a company together at the just-right dimensions to allow things to go on indefinitely.
2. Sustainability is the watchword, an implied Sustainability of Ethical Responsibility.
3. AI: Robot is not a fancy toy but as computers came in, fear removed and used by all now, AI is most welcome. It can be put to better use.
4. The board of directors: "To gain advantage in the future, the current generation of organizational leaders should look to Sustainable Value System in their companies, #AI will be of no help."
5. Reverse mentoring: The components are there, what is needed is an integration of Qualitative and Quantitative elements, to breathe into a business entity in human form. Reverse mentoring will happen, and the seniors shall not ignore it.

Notes

1. NASA. https://spaceplace.nasa.gov/sun-age/en/.
2. UN Documents. n.d. "Report of the World Commission on Environment and Development: Our Common Future." http://www.un-documents.net/ocf-ov.htm#I.
3. KPMG. 2018. "Rethinking the Value Chain: A Study on AI, Humanoids and Robots." https://assets.kpmg/content/dam/kpmg/xx/pdf/2018/09/rethinking-the-value-chain.pdf.
4. KPMG. 2018. "Rethinking the Value Chain.": https://assets.kpmg/content/dam/kpmg/xx/pdf/2018/09/rethinking-the-value-chain.pdf.
5. IBEF. 2020. "Agriculture in India: Information About Indian Agriculture and Its Importance." https://www.ibef.org/industry/agriculture-india.aspx.
6. Ibid.; J. Iyer. 2019. "One Page Report Project Fiscal." https://www.linkedin.com/posts/jayaraman-iyer-6027b71_one-page-report-project-fiscal-activity-6526499813792538624-caQL.
7. Source: FAOSTAT via http://www.factfish.com/.
8. Source: World Bank via http://www.factfish.com/.
9. World Bank. http://wdi.worldbank.org/table/4.2; Economic Times. 2020. "Agriculture Has Key Role in Making India $5 Trillion Economy: PM Modi." https://economictimes.indiatimes.com/news/economy/agriculture/agriculture-has-key-role-in-making-india-5-trillion-economy-pm-modi/articleshow/73072838.cms?utm_source=contentofinterest&utm_medium=text&utm_campaign=cppst.
10. This quote is from Cosmos by C. Sagan. https://www.goodreads.com/quotes/117588-every-one-of-us-is-in-the-cosmic-perspective-precious.

CHAPTER 8

The CEO Practices and CREAM Report for Corporate Electron

You can't connect the dots, looking forward, you can only connect them looking backward. So, you have to trust that the dots will somehow connect in your future.

—Steve Jobs*

There are three issue areas in connecting the dots between the past and the future. First, the past is presented in the analysis of Hindustan Unilever Limited (HUL), a subsidiary of Unilever (UL), in a CREAM Report made up of corporate governance, risk management, earnings, accounting quality, and management quality. This report provides the basis of CREAM Analytics. Second, a brief outline of the Capital-Output ratio related to India's growth targets and vision for a $5 trillion economy by 2024 is presented. Growth targets estimated need to be tracked with the help of a CREAM Report. Third, a CREAM Report for Strategy Plan 2024 is taken up. Converting CAGR and CARR into CDGR, CDRR respectively that is going to play a major role in tracking the goals set. The fault lines of the past, challenges of the present, and the effort to the future under CEO practices, the electron, exemplify the need to arrest management failures that companies currently face. As mentioned in earlier chapters, the corporate electron spins around the nucleus that contains the board, policies, and regulatory bodies. Given the right mix and the capability of individuals, there's no reason to disbelieve that a corporate renaissance would emerge.

---

*https://news.stanford.edu/2005/06/14/jobs-061505/

CREAM Report - HUL

Data from 2007 to 2018–19 is analyzed. For the convenience of presentation in a book format, we consider the two years 2007 and 2008-09, and then three years 2016-17, 2017-18 and the latest annual report 2018-19, skipping the intermediate years. The two tables provided in Chapter 7 indicate 1. Index of inactivity (IA) by Process Area and 2. IA by Resource Area. The data is derived from the published annual reports of HUL from 2007 to 2018-19. The data provided here is a consolidated figure of the CREAM Report, totaling 170 Process Blocks. One of the categories, management quality, has 98 combining 97 + 1(19) Process Blocks, with 19 Blocks compressed into 1. These are open-ended Process Blocks that vary from company to company, but the core issue areas are well covered and are applicable to all companies. Management quality (98) consists of the following:

1. Board of Directors (9)
2. Audit Committee (13)
3. Nomination and Remuneration Committee (9)
4. Reward Policy (12)
5. Stakeholders' Relationship Committee (3)
6. CSR and other functional committees (7)
7. UL CoBP (19)
8. HUL CoBP (7)
9. Preventing Conflict of Interests (7)
10. Whistleblower Policy (5)
11. Share Dealing Code (4)
12. UN Global Compact (3)

Total Issue Areas (98)

    IA (Table 7.1) by Process Area reveals the CREAM details. The total of Active + Inactive elements represents the total number of Process Blocks handled during the respective year. At the optimized level of performance, each gets valued 5. With 5 people for each process, it would be 25. The total number of Process Blocks is 152 in the first two years and 151 in the last three years; multiplication by 25 gets the total number of points 3,800 or 3,775 as the case may be.

Earnings: Each category is independently assessed, block by block. In the case of earnings, they are calculated as per the profitability statement and the balance sheet but brought to the same ratings as in Table 5.2, at a standard of 15 percent CAGR. Earnings are the only quantitative element, with 12 Process Blocks, which are fair representations to understand how the company is doing. Yet IA percent for the same runs from 59.33 percent to 70.00 percent, which is high. IA percent ideally should be 0 percent, to confirm that what is targeted, is achieved. When 59.33 percent is the IA percent, then the fault lines are high as well as it reveals that the standard 15 percent CAGR is unachievable. In order to reduce the IA percent from 59.33 percent, more effort is called for. One of the major contributors to this high IA percent in earnings is the ratio of Employee Benefits per day to Sales per day. Not in a single year, is the ratio anywhere near the target of 15 percent. This means the company performance of employees is below par. So is the case with Advertising and Promotion Expenses.

Per day sales: Annual Accounts for 2007 were by the calendar year, that is, 365 days. Whereas in 2008–2009, the number of days was 457, since the annual accounting year was extended by another quarter to change the accounting year, as per country rules. However, the number of days is considered to calculate the daily sales for each year, variation being whether it is a leap year or not. This is the main principle behind CAGR converted into CDGR or CARR into CDRR. Also, the basis of IBCM (see Chapter 6) is "Activity has a cost incidence whereas Inactivity a cost consequence. Measure Cost Consequence, Now, Now, Now." First, quarterly reports and annual reports are of no use to this end. Second, decisions made need to be tracked with immediacy, on a daily basis. We start a project and delegate without a proper tracking system in place. Per day changes have to be tracked vis-à-vis the targets set. Management quality has 98 Process Blocks, none of which are tracked. Infosys is currently engaged in firefighting work on its whistleblower policy, which is one of the 98 under the aforementioned management quality. On a single day, on October 21, 2019, the U.S.-listed American Depository Receipts (ADRs) of the IT major Infosys fell 15.7 percent, according to news reports.[1] A Big 4 multinational professional services firm, a legal firm, and the audit committee of Infosys are entrusted with unraveling whistleblower complaints. Corporate Governance is a dynamic function. The number of Process Blocks shown for corporate governance in Table 7.1 Index of Inactivity by Process Area is 19, whereas management quality is 98. Companies neither take action on such policies they have created nor report on them. Ideally, corporate governance issue areas must be more than what is stated under management quality. Each must be brought under return on intangible rating system, daily.

The same info by Process Areas is created by Resource Area (see Table 7.2).

In the context of past results being analyzed, fiscal responsibility is equally shared, whereas ethical responsibility is given independently for each Process Block. Although one may get the impression that past results cannot be detected for either of the responsibilities, return on intangible helps to identify fault lines. The Six Stages of Transformation to Substance helps. One can identify a whistleblower policy created with Quality, by its full marks, a rating of 5, whereas when left abandoned as a "read, laughed, filed code," it's 0. So Intellectual Value Capital is 5 and Action Value Capital is 0, resulting in an Intangible Value Capital of 2. An Intangible Value Capital of 2 is a disaster for any company with IA of 60 percent.

The 98 Process Blocks in management quality have three issue areas being discussed conflict of interest, conflict of personal interest, and conflict of conscience. Normally, steps are taken for the first one with board members giving information in advance of interested parties they are related to. On the other hand, conflict of personal interest is difficult to catch, despite established insider trading rules. In the case of conflicts of interest versus conflicts of personal interest, one prevents participation and the other urges nonparticipation. But as they say, "No gentleman is a hero to his valet." The culprit is identified by some close contacts within a company. *Arthapatti* (presumption or implication) can help, for there must be a *linga* (form or symbol), like smoke from fire, thunder from clouds, which leaves a clue. Conflict of conscience arises for people who easily find smoke where there is not even a spark of a fire. They are part of the whistleblowing community. To them, the absence of evidence is not evidence of absence. Their contribution to Corporate Ethical Assets is truly great but never acknowledged.

Capital–Output Ratio

China in 2005 had a GDP of $2.285 trillion. It reached $5.109 trillion by 2009. That is a CAGR of 22.28 percent in four years. If India has to grow from $2.75 trillion in 2018 to $5 trillion in 2024, the CAGR would be 16.12 percent. The current growth rate is waning but for the 2014 to 2018 years,[2] there has been a steady growth at 7 percent. To understand Capital–Output Ratio, suppose investment is 32 percent (of GDP) and the economic growth corresponding to this level of investment is 8 percent, Capital–Output Ratio is 32/8 or 4. If the expected growth rate for next year is 9 percent, then the level of investment needs to increase from 32 to 36 (9 × 4). Capital–Output Ratio becomes the relationship between the level of investment and the corresponding economic growth. China could expand fast in four years mainly on account of infusion of foreign direct investment (FDI), whereas India did not get its share. "India contributes nearly 3% of the world's GDP but has only a 1% share of global investment money. If this figure were to just double to 2%, that would mean nearly $3 trillion of investments flowing into India,"[3] says Prem Watsa, of Fairfax Financial Holdings, Canada.

That apart, what is crucial is the Capital–Output Ratio. If it is 3 instead of 4, when the investment is 32 percent, then the growth rate is 10.67 percent (32/3) and 12 if investment reaches 36 percent. With underutilized capacity and investments already made, corporate needs increased productivity from each sector. For example, India stands second in the hierarchy of agriculture for all countries, per data 2017, at $401.32 billion. The same year, India's GDP stood at $2597.49 billion. This is about 15.45 percent. Between 1960 and 1988, China and India were neck and neck in agri production. From 1989 onward, China galloped, achieving 2.87 times India's growth in the year 2015.[4] China had left India far behind. India has a lot of catching up to do. On the one hand, FDIs in agriculture would be most welcome. So far, FDI in agri is pretty meager.[5] (FDI in India's food processing sector, for example, stood at $628.24 million in 2018–19.) On the other hand, yield should take precedence over investments if Capital–Output Ratio has to improve.

This is the critical aspect of management of corporate or agriculture—better utilization of investments. "Agriculture is the primary source of livelihood for about 58 percent of India's population. Gross Value Added by agriculture, forestry, and fishing is estimated at Rs 18.53 trillion (US$ 271.00 billion) in FY18, as per IBEF study."[6] Being a single large sector, it is agriculture, more than corporate India, that would trigger the race toward a $5 trillion Indian economy by 2024. Though neglected over several decades, farmer producer organisations (FPOs) and farmer producer companies (FPCs) are well structured and accommodate millions of farmers. Each FPO is made up of about 1,000 farmers and each farmer buys a share @Rs1,000 ($14.29), making it an FPO company with a share capital of Rs10 lakhs ($14,285/). For example, Gujpro Agri-business Consortium Producer Company, Gujarat, has about 30 FPOs under its supervision, covering 40,000 farmers. There are hundreds of such FPOs in India. In the 2019 budget, Finance Minister Nirmala Sitharaman proposed to create a minimum of 10,000 FPOs that would cover about 13 million farmers. Unlike corporate that indulges in killing competition, FPOs share their problems, help each other, and are ready to listen. Investments in agriculture in India will raise the productivity index sufficiently to compete with China, in turn increasing the scope for returns. Return on intangible applied to individual FPOs could transform the whole agri sector toward prosperity with exports. Farmers' groups are willing to introduce Fairtrade, HACCP, Agri Codex, and various other ethical standards in their units. Basically, Indian farmers have maintained their tradition of honesty and integrity even at their own cost and peril. Such measures would help reduce the tragedy of farmer suicides.

Strategy Plan Is Declaring That a Company Is Binding Their Commitment Deeper, with a CREAM Report

The Six Stages of Transformation to Substance, from the thinking stage to a Strategy Plan in 2024, needs to take place in every company, and mainly in startups. To continue to do the same thing, will earn only the same results. The new strategy is measuring by cost consequence now, now, now, which brings to limelight the decisions taken today are tracked to their efficacy then and there. Corporate Atomic Structure facilitates an organized decision-making capability by clear-cut responsibility in the first instance and tracked with return on intangible for accountability, performance, nonperformance, and self-governance.

Keeping a $5 trillion Indian economy and its growth rates in focus, let each corporate and agri sector prepare a Strategy Plan with clarity on sustainability of Efficiency, sustainability of Value System, and sustainability of Profits, establishing growth rates and reduction rates, CAGR, and CARR. The crucial aspect of the exercise would be to arrive at the National Grid of Governance by each company being connected to each other. Return on intangible is a formula created for assessing performance as well as nonperformance of each individual. Participants need to exchange data and help each other to raise their company's ratings from the current status to the targeted optimized level. To set CAGR much higher than it is now will depend on the optimized performances of individual companies. Tasks schedules, like project management, a series of tasks by respective series of Time, should be entrusted to respective individuals, by a series of Dates. For example, in New Delhi currently, there is a proposal cleared for the massive revamp of Rajpath (which is a ceremonial boulevard in New Delhi), construction of a new Parliament and central secretariat—a plan that aims at creating a new office district for several ministries and offices. The work would be spread over the next four years. The contractor company would be better served by their team targeting 2024 with CDGR starting now. Tracking the project daily with an Index of Inactivity by several process areas and more importantly by resource area would go to establish progress at all fronts. The Strategy Plan 2024 would cover CREAM Report contents in all respects.

Spot Your Place

Establish a connection between yourself and the $5 trillion Indian economy. Establish a connection between the $5 trillion economy and all countries above India's GDP—France, the United Kingdom, Germany, Japan, China, and the United States. Spot your place today and what you want to be four years hence. Analyze the CREAM Report of each company and check what it adds up to in the Indian economy. Spotting your place seems pretty tiny for a startup. India has a tradition of chanting a *sankalpa* on every New Moon day. A *sankalpa* is nothing more than an intention—a solemn vow, determination, or will. In practical terms, a *sankalpa* means a one-pointed resolve to focus both psychologically and philosophically on a specific goal. In addition, the sacred practitioners declare where they are in the context of time. They start from the Big Bang and list the time that has elapsed since then until today's date, calculating step by step, and arriving at the day by identifying oneself with the universe. The same commitment is expected for any company to relate itself with all countries above India's own GDP. If you must be an ant, be an atom ant. These are the building blocks of CREAM Reports, constructing values and deconstructing the valueless, that connect to the $5 trillion Indian economy on a daily basis.

Ethical Assets Premium Account

It is proposed that every Management Quality Process Block having a number of Quality principles, such as UNGC or UNCAC or CoBP, has a debit and credit account for it. For example, on account of one quality policy document, such as CoBP, a notional value of Rs1 crore ($142,850/-) will be debited to the Ethical Assets Account and the same amount credited to the Ethical Assets Premium Account, subject to fulfilling certain conditions. The condition being that CoBP will be certified by a certification agency or the auditor of the company according to the ratings obtained, as per Table 5.2. If ratings are at the optimized level of 5, then 100 percent of the notional value gets debited and correspondingly credited to the premium account. FPOs, made up of ordinary farmers, are designed to have a small value share capital. However there are several ethical assets FPOs possess, such as the code of agribusiness practices, Fairtrade, HACCP, CoC. Once say four such ethical assets are monetized, the premium account value is bound to be substantial, for each FPO. An FPC is made up of several FPOs. The ethical assets premium account would surpass their collective share capital many a time since many FPOs operate under a single FPC. It would help an FDI to immediately track the Ethical Values followed by a company while committing their investments. The same Ethical Assets Account for a major corporate vis-à-vis the auditor involved, anything less than 100 percent, could be a disaster on their corporate governance leadership. The likes of IL&FS would never arise if the Ethical Assets Premium Account is monitored on a daily basis. For such companies, it is not too late to start the creation of an Ethical Assets Account now.

Chapter 8: Points to Ponder

1. Connecting the dots: Past, present, and future need to be connected, in a systematic manner. Past is to correct the fault lines; present is the opportunity to state that our dreams have to be bigger - set our ambitions higher - binding our commitment deeper, and then move forward to the future - to exert our efforts greater. This is a step-by-step successive advancement from strategy idea to strategy planning to strategy plan to strategy action.

2. CREAM Report of HUL with an overall IA by Process Area and Resource Area explains the intricacies of preparing and using data for corporate governance, risk management, earnings, accounting quality, and management quality analytics. Differentiating conflicts of interest, conflicts of personal interest, and conflicts of conscience adds spice to the menu. CREAM Report highlights how qualitative elements of management are far greater than the quantitative elements of management, that it is no surprise when 85 percent of corporate management is not measured or tracked. Principle #1—what gets measured, gets managed—is a true statement.

3. Capital - Output Ratio underlines our need to reach out to the $5 trillion Indian economy, the ingredients for successful productivity, and how the return on intangible would be necessary. Agri sector is elaborated with FPOs and FPCs participating in a major revolution for increased GDP being a homogenous unit, and they are collectively better than corporate to handle and contribute. The crucial point of observation is the willingness of the farmers to cooperate, help each other, embrace standards, and increase yields, which would aid meeting the targets attracting FDIs.

4. Strategy Plan - binding our commitment deeper - CREAM Report is the time to commit on paper a strategy plan for the future. Future is brought to present as CAGR and CARR are converted

into CDGR and CDRR, which are Daily controls to track the decisions made today and checked today itself.
5. Spot your place is to identify a startup to reach out to the stars. Connecting the dots means startup, to the related sector, Indian $5 trillion economy, challenge China is in straight line, enabling a tiny industrious individual to relate to the global economy.
6. The importance of Qualitative Elements of management, which make up the Ethical Assets, is highlighted as how to measure and how to create Ethical Assets Premium Account. This is crucial for corporate as well as audit firms to buck up.
7. The electron - CEO team - is the most visible aspect of corporate management. Brought under control by the nucleus of a Corporate Atomic Structure, containing the stakeholders, it delineates the duty, responsibility, and accountability.

Action Point

1. Leadership "is not about giving energy, but unleashing others' people energy"; leadership is the electron of the Corporate Atomic Structure.
2. A $5 trillion Indian economy in 2024 from the 2018 $2.75 trillion at a CAGR of 16.12 percent should have a breakup of all major GDP contributors—agriculture, energy, infrastructure construction, trade, hotels, tourism, transport, storage, communication, banking, financing, insurance, real estate, business services, community, social and personal services, and so on—with individual CAGR from the start-up levels. Then convert to CDGR for each unit of the building blocks, and then track the progress from today's $2.75 trillion to the $5 trillion target, Daily.
3. Looking at Whistleblower policy and the FCPA, one is protective and the other intends to punish ex post facto, but neither of them is proactive. Change the denominator.

Notes

1. BusinessToday.In. 2019. "Infosys US-Listed Shares Tumble 16% after Whistleblower Complaints." https://www.businesstoday.in/markets/company-stock/infosys-us-listed-shares-tumble-16-after-whistleblower-complaints/story/385969.html.
2. The World Bank. https://data.worldbank.org/indicator/NY.GDP.MKTP.KD.ZG?locations=IN.
3. M. Bhalla. 2019. "Fairfax to Invest $5 Billion More in India in Next 5 Years." https://economictimes.indiatimes.com/news/economy/finance/fairfax-to-invest-5-billion-morein-india-in-next-5-years/articleshow/70942015.cms.
4. World Bank. n.d. "Agriculture, Forestry, and Fishing, Value Added (current US$)," World Bank national accounts data, and OECD National Accounts data files. https://data.worldbank.org/indicator/NV.AGR.TOTL.CD.
5. IBEF. 2020. "Indian Agriculture and Allied Industries Industry Report." https://www.ibef.org/industry/agriculture-india.aspx.
6. Ibid.

CHAPTER 9

Society for Corporate Neutron

Every atom is made from three kinds of elementary particles, where Neutrons have no charge. Neutrons don't influence an atom's identity, but they do add to its mass.

—Bill Bryson*

Knowledge is the goal of ethics. In the classificatory scheme of conformability with nature, society forms a nucleus. In the case of corporate, this is with the board, and in case of government, with the constitution. Society does not influence the identity of the Corporate Atomic Structure or the Governmental Atomic Structure but adds mass to them. Society can vote out a government, can shut a factory like Sterilite, can put a lid on a product like the mercury thermometer. It is society that is being influenced, not the other way. Society is a powerful ally whose freedom of thought is limited by the constraints imposed by a few, corporate or government. Mahatma Gandhi could influence humanity as a whole with the message of self-governance. The greatness of Gandhi lay in channeling the waves of anger of a mob toward disciplined demands for the society. Society is part of the nucleus, as the neutron. Memorandum and articles of association for corporate and constitution for government are the protons. CEO team for corporate, and judiciary, executive, and legislative functions for the government are electrons. As part of the nucleus, society provides stability to the Corporate/Government Atomic Structure and prevents the electrons from spinning too fast and going off tangent. In order to do so, it alters the executive part of electrons as the need arises. In fact, the power conferred on corporate and government is at the initiative and approval of the society. Indian culture is based on accepting and

---

*A Short History of Nearly Everything

conducting both of these with Ethical Responsibility. This rule helps allies of society. Return on intangible is a do it yourself (DIY) kit.

Society teaches in different ways, violent, nonviolent, revolution, or by a strenuous process of explication of laws. The first three are by mass movement whereas the last one by government looking into the finer aspect of society's demands. Many companies do not wait for laws to be enacted to follow certain basic principles like the Code of Good Conduct or the CoBP. However, for the same set of companies when profit motive becomes the greatest urgency, the ethical indifference overrides the ethical seriousness. Understanding and undertaking of the ethical responsibility consistently and persistently, is going to be the coherent corporate management operating system, post-COVID-19, practices.

Transparency is lost with ethical indifference toward the society. Rules, whether mandatory or otherwise, express ethical motives. Compliance with the rules and informing the public by UNCAC Article 10, Public Reporting, is the transparency. Transparency justifies companies' conduct, which is the societal good. The goal of ethical motive is the knowledge of societal good. Accumulation and retention of such knowledge is the goal of ethics.

This work is on sustainability. Multibillion-dollar investments and acquisitions need to be created carefully in six stages of the Creative Process. A hierarchical one-man call center is no more. Strategy Plan is ready, means it is a Quality Substance. Risk factors, as had swept away the feet of Volkswagen and Bayer, ought to have been brought up during the Creative Process, stage 5 – Formulation - and discussed threadbare, including UNCAC Article 13, Participation of Society. This relates to ego discrimination in the third stage of Pascal's mental evolution. This work explains in detail the bottom-to-top structuring of operations with the foot soldier as the VIP. The intention is Strategy Plan is of the managerial force whereas Action Process relates to the work performed by every individual. One important aspect of this work is that there are no separate ratings for a company, but combined ratings of individuals go for the company's ratings. It means a single task from a multimillion number of tasks is tracked to a single individual. It means Accountability is embedded. Together transparency and accountability form the knowledge base, arising out of ethical standards adopted. The knowledge base is empty now. Fill her up with Corporate Hydrogen and accelerate!

Just and equitable society: Author and historian H.G. Wells said, "Amidst the tens of thousands of names of monarchs that crowd the columns of history ... the name of Ashoka shines, and shines almost alone, a star." Ashoka's regime, around 300 BC, was characteristic of ethical responsibility undertaken by the people and the government. This ethical responsibility undertaken then should be of intense scrutiny and application now. Civilization is always on the move, claiming the recent one is better than the previous one. What truly typified Ashoka's regime was the set of rules that expressed the truth and by following it up it ensured the conduct, of all. In the meantime, colonization of East Asian countries, particularly India, has deprived the civilization to move up but brought it down with the blind philosophy of "He that is not with me is against me, and he that gathereth not with me, scattereth." The result is obvious: Modern civilization is bereft of any ethical values. The contents of Ashoka's edicts justify some of the legends about his wise and humane rule, qualifying him to be ranked as one of the world's greatest rulers at a time when Europe was in the dark ages and America didn't exist. Knowledge of how Ashoka's regime catered to society is an eye-opener on Ethical Responsibility undertaken and fulfilled.

Ashoka's edicts speak of what might be called "state morality" and private or individual morality. The first was what he based his administration on and what he hoped would lead to a more just, more spiritually inclined society. The second was what he recommended and encouraged individuals to practice. Ashoka's edicts are the age-old and time-tested Substance of Quality and Action, proven effective in running a humane society. The following steps, taken and implemented by his regime, are well described by Ven. S. Dhammika[1]:

1. State morality and private or individual morality
2. Policy of peaceful coexistence
3. Reform of the judicial system
4. Utilization of state resources for useful public works
5. Accessibility to the ruler, Ashoka
6. Welfare of its people
7. Human rights - compassion, moderation, tolerance, and respect for all life
8. Animal rights
9. Protection of all religions
10. Generosity to the poor
11. Well-learned in the good doctrines of other people's religions

The edicts, carved into stone all over India, were instrumental in creating a just and equitable society, long before we are attempting to do so now. *The 11 challenges we observe from Ashoka's edicts are valid today, rather more so today, particularly the eleventh.* Such a society is possible only if we get our equation right, and if the accountability of each member of the teams entrusted with implementing these 11 edicts, is tracked. It's not just responsibility but co-responsibility. Change the denominator.

Gross National Happiness [GNH] Index

I Happiness Index

Continuing with Ashoka's edicts, the 11 Critical Control Points of Societal Good and Ethical Conduct, let us look into the Happiness Index as a primary tool for assessing and measuring state and individual happiness. (State morality, private or individual morality, Ashoka's #1.) The following reports are perused to highlight the Global Happiness Index–related work.

1. The 2019 *Global Happiness and Wellbeing Policy Report* is a landmark survey of the state of global happiness that ranks 156 countries by how happy their citizens perceive themselves to be. The report is produced by the United Nations Sustainable Development Solutions Network in partnership with the Ernesto Illy Foundation.[2]
2. The 2019 *World Happiness Report*[3]
3. "Happiness: Toward a Holistic Approach to Development," Draft note, November 6, 2012: Author Luis.Collantes.[4]
4. "Gross National Happiness vs Gross Domestic Product"[5]

On a comparative note, on 170 process blocks of the HUL case study given in Chapter 8, one can identify the nature of the process blocks of a manufacturing and marketing organization. These are open-ended process blocks, meaning if one does not find some of the critical areas of analysis and measurement, then one is bound to add a few more. Please note, first, as mentioned in our CREAM Report findings stated earlier, there are no separate company ratings, but individual ratings combine to produce overall ratings for the organization. Second and more importantly, a process block is identical to any other process block, thanks to Newton's Laws of

Motion. Process blocks are restricted to policies created and practices acted upon for any company. Normally a company does not include Happiness Index as part of a corporate operating system. Now happiness index can be added as a process block for each issue area, by a written policy and can be measured as to how they are practiced. One such process block group is a Happiness Index, which is not integrated into many companies as such, let alone HUL. Some of the important issue areas of each industry group these provisions can be added as process blocks. Process blocks are restricted to policies created and practices acted upon for any company. Normally a company does not include Happiness Index as part of a corporate operating system. Now happiness index can be added as a process block for each issue area, by written policy and can be measured as to how they are practiced. Happiness Index forms a considerable number of process blocks. The Global Council for Happiness and Wellbeing (GCHW) lists such process blocks under the following categories:

1. Health
2. Education
3. Work
4. Personal Happiness
5. Cities

HUL, for example, may add all the five issue areas, as part of their CSR and Sustainable Living Plan schemes. Happiness Index for these categories would fall under nonmandatory provisions, like the Code of Good Conduct. With the detailed provisions made available by "Happiness: Towards a Holistic Approach to Development," there is no dearth of rules that would go to measure the Happiness Index.

II Ranking in the *World Happiness Report* for 156 countries is based on certain metrics and criteria. This is an annual report that possibly induces the desire of almost all countries to know where they are placed from the previous year. From the report prepared in 2012, quote:[6]
Moreover, most conclusions of "happiness surveys" are usually based on information from WEIRD (Western, educated, industrialized, rich democracies) countries, limiting their credibility. In addition, people's aspirations and standards change and there may be a happiness set point depending on an individual. Lastly, there are lingering

doubts about taking happiness seriously. With much hardship, poverty, disease, war, and crime in existence, focusing on happiness may seem a luxury. Unquote. The doubts raised remain valid, even now.

III GDP: In the same 2012 report conclusions were drawn thus: In general terms, governments are encouraged to (1) recognize that GDP is not the only indicator of well-being, (2) integrate economic and social policies better, (3) develop specific policies for environmental protection, and (4) develop well-being indicators to guide their policy design and monitoring in line with sustainable development objectives.

IV GNH: In the paper "GNH vs GDP" the author quotes His Majesty Jigme Singye Wangchuck, the Fourth King of Bhutan: "Gross National Happiness is more important than Gross National Product."

Since long sustainability development has progressed well to specify like 10 Principles in four issue areas of the UNGC, United Nations Millennium Declaration of sustainability of economic, social, environmental protection, and development goals. However, points raised in the UN Draft Note of 2012 remain unresolved. Use of GDP figures is a constant reminder of delay and undependability of statistics. For example, an extract from the 2019 *Global Happiness and Wellbeing Policy Report* says, "GDP data for 2018 are not yet available, so we extend the GDP time series from 2017 to 2018 using country-specific forecasts of real GDP growth from the OECD Economic Outlook No. 104 (Edition November 2018) and the World Bank's Global Economic Prospects (Last Updated: 06/07/2018), after adjustment for population growth."

What could be concluded is that the Happiness Index cannot be integrated into GDP data mainly due to the delay it poses whereas GNH data can be processed in a better time frame. GNH has many indicators that can be used effectively, but the WEIRD syndrome persists, with the result the Global Happiness Index is not taken seriously.

V Integrate GDP and GNH: GDP is crucial to track Sustainability development issues of economic, social, environmental protection, and development goals. Under the holistic approach of overall economic development, the other goals could be met. The link to GDP shall be maintained by GNH or the Happiness Index. GDP data needs to be thoroughly overhauled. A stand-alone GNH not linked with GDP data is tantamount to corporate producing results sans profitability/balance sheet details. We do try to fix the corporate balance sheet comprehensively, but GDP stats needing complete overhaul needs attention.

Efforts per person [EPP] ~ GDP

Recently I have been requested by the president of the Federation of Industries and Associations (FIA) Gujarat to prepare a blueprint for the GSDP of $1.5 trillion, 2024. FIA at Gandhinagar is one of the foremost and active associations of Gujarat having 202 industry associations and around 150,000 industrial units as its members. The FIA plays an active role in representing issues faced by industries under the Gujarat Industrial Development Corporation (GIDC), Industries Commissionarate, Industrial Extension Bureau (IndexTb), Gujarat Pollution Control Board (GPCB), Goods and Services Tax (GST), Customs, and so on and suggests policy issues to the state and central governments. Currently, I am an adviser for CDGR and of Ethics Committee. I did prepare a blueprint in January 2020 on the basis of this work principle of CAGR and CDGR. Some salient features of GSDP $1.5 trillion in 2024 and what one encounters in preparing such a GDP analysis:

1. Only one document STATE DOMESTIC PRODUCT GUJARAT STATE 2017–2018 (With Base Year 2011–2012), one could get. This document was prepared a few months earlier, on September 4, 2019, with 2016–2017 stated as P—Provisional—and 2017–2018 stated as Q - Quick Estimates. General talk about the GSDP was said to be $250 billion currently. The $1.5 trillion 2024 seemed quite achievable, so the chief minister of Gujarat had started announcing the target of $1.5 trillion by 2024 in very many public forums.
2. At the end of January 2020 when the *Economic Survey of India* 2019–2020 was presented in Parliament, Table 1.10A. Net State Domestic Product, State/UT stats for the year 2018 - 2019[7] contained n/a to indicate not applicable to very many states, including Gujarat and Maharashtra, for 2018–2019. The fault lines on the preparation of GSDP are apparent, going at a leisurely pace between a state and the central stats. They are 2 years off the target year stats. One can imagine how this would be extended to World Bank or OECD stats.

3. The blueprint for GSDP $1.5 trillion by 2024, therefore, took cognizance of this lacunae and advised how to go ahead with Strategy Plan 2024 for $1.5 trillion. There were two parts to the Strategy Plan 2024, one Creative Process and two Action Process. First, the Creative Process took detailed information of six stages of development of a Strategy Plan 2024, as now the readers are familiar with. Second, the details of IBCM - where Activity has a cost incidence and Inactivity a Cost Consequence, Measure Cost Consequence Now, Now, Now - have been brought to focus. This is to emphasize the futility of preparing GSDP coming out with figures that are 3 to 4 years old if one looks at the provisional and quick estimates periods. So, the blueprint emphasized the need for developing Strategy Plan 2024 (i) with a CAGR of 2024 for all the Industry Group within GSDP 2018 - 2024 and (ii) convert it into CDGR for action process daily, tracking the set targets and daily performance thereon.

4. GSDP/CAGR: GSDP rose from Rs 615,606 crores ($87.94 billion) in 2012 to Rs.1,314,680 crores ($187.81 billion) in 2018, at a CAGR of 11.45 percent in 7 years. For the same period per capita has grown at a CAGR of 10.20 percent.

    For the same period per capita has grown at a CAGR of 10.20 percent. Extending the same from 2018 to 2024, the target of $1.5 trillion in 6 years would amount to a CAGR of 41.38 percent.

    GSDP 2018–2024 is based on projection at CAGR of 41.38 percent. The GSDP 2024 targets $1.50 trillion. There are natural variations in CAGR 2012–2018 at varying rates for industry group. CAGR of 41.38 percent is applied uniformly to each sectoral industry. The variation between 2012–2018 CAGR and 2024 CAGR for each industry group signifies the effort to be put in to compete uniformly to reach the target of GSDP $1.5 trillion in 2024.

5. There are two aspects to the setting of targets for the state of Gujarat at 41.38 percent. One is that it is comparable to South Korea - in area Gujarat is 195% percent of South Korea, in population Gujarat is 1.17 times of South Korea, and in GDP Gujarat is just 12 percent of South Korea (South Korea GDP $1.5 trillion and Gujarat $187.81 billion). In principle and with effort Gujarat is placed in a position to challenge South Korea to achieve the targeted $1.5 trillion. The second aspect of setting such a steep target is Gujarat is an entrepreneurial state with

vibrant people. Who are you? The second chapter of this work has a lot to bear for Gujaratis, who can set a stiff target and yet achieve it.

6. EPP - efforts per person: (Figure 9.1) The principle behind this book is return on intangible. This book explains in detail the bottom-to-top structuring of operations with the foot soldier as the VIP. Table 7.1, Index of Inactivity by Process Area, and Table 7.2, Index of Inactivity by Resource Area, tally the efforts put in by each individual, by each process area, as to the targets set and achieved. By the same principle, the following figure represents the EPP on the GSDP $1.5 trillion 2024 targets.

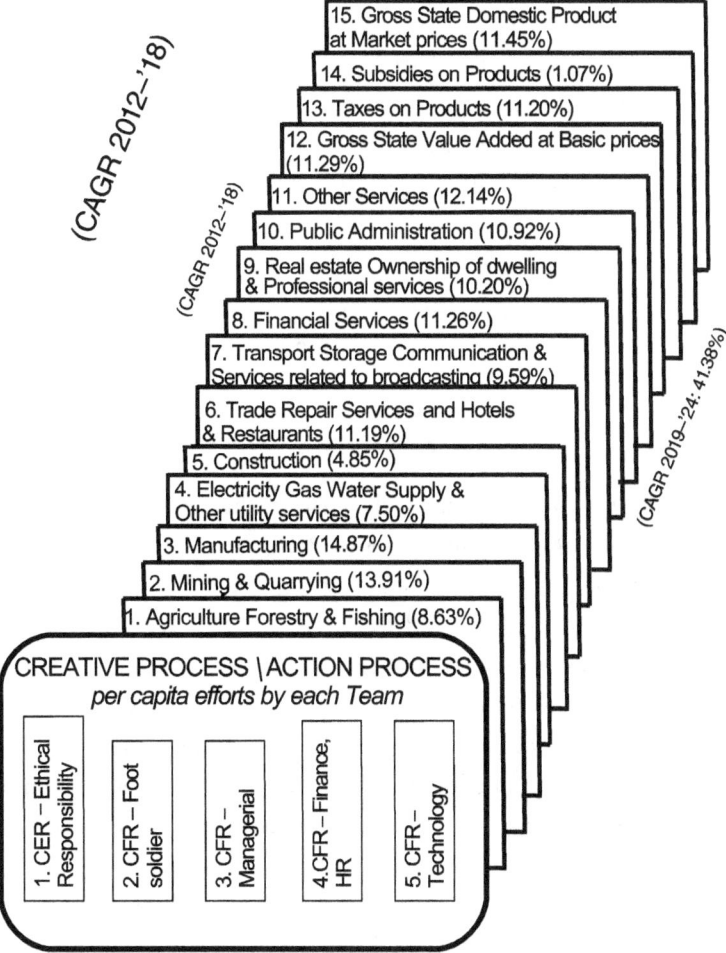

Figure 9.1 *EPP - efforts per person*

Both the Creative Process and the Action Process need work inputs to target the set 41.38 percent CAGR by 2024. Individual industry group's current average is given. In the same manner as in Tables 7.1 and 7.2, for each unit representing part of GSDP targets, EPP needs to be prepared. By Process Area as well as by Resource Area an IA would give the targets set at 41.38 percent for each industry group and performance as on today, covering the entire GSDP target of $1.5 trillion. In cricket parlance, it is like playing a one day international (ODI), where the dashboard displays current run rate as against the expected run rate set as target. The entire $1.5 trillion economy would be tracked on a daily basis by CDGR. Individual units in each industry group would bring about the needed work performance to reach the set targets. The dashboard would display the EPP score of each person, then the team, then the organization, then the industry group, and in total the GSDP 2024.

There are two aspects to a CREAM Report: One is the Quantitative element of management represented by E - earnings. Collectively, the fiscal assets growth and utilization that would go to add up the GSDP or GDP; another, Qualitative elements of management represented by CRAM - corporate governance, risk management, accounting quality, and management quality. Collectively, the Ethical Assets representing the set of rules and justifying the conduct would add up the GNH.

Both GDP and GNH go together; not one versus the other.

Creamchain

If the description of knowledge is the goal of ethics, it is said transparency and accountability form the knowledge base, arising out of ethical standards adopted. As stated earlier, knowledge base is empty now; fill it up with Corporate Hydrogen and accelerate.

EPP should bring up the transparency and accountability factors to the fore, then the knowledge base gets some data. The important aspect of what society wants to hear is accountability. In the case of *Economic Survey* 2019 - 2020, it was observed some of the data under the current year was mentioned as n/a. Normally it means not applicable. Quite strange indeed! However, from the point of view of society, it is NOT ACCEPTABLE. The data explosion is said to be huge. The information explosion is the rapid increase in the amount of published information or data and the effects of this abundance. As suggested in creating GDP from the bottom-to-top, data is identifiable to a single person. For example, farmers' work brought up through the FPOs and FPCs, without in any way ignoring the effort put in by a single farmer. Hence, EPP data is going to be decisive in the success of entire global data management. In a World Bank or OECD report on GDP the components can be traced back to the building blocks of each industry group and then to each individual who had put in effort to build the block. CREAM Report provides the data necessary to build a GDP and GNH stats.

Blockchain can be of great help. Blockchain is another technology one should use but not misuse. The National Institute of Standards and Technology (NIST) has published a paper on Blockchain Technology Overview.[8] Under the head "Tamper-Evident and Tamper-Resistant Data," it says, "Many applications follow the "CRUD" (create, read, update, delete) functions for data. With a blockchain, there is only "CR" (create, read). There are methods that can be employed to "deprecate" older data if a newer version is found, but there is no removal process for the original data."

This book provides the basis for creating a CREAM Report for companies. CREAM Report and Blockchain, combined, establish ratings for a National Grid of Governance. More importantly, an individual with a blockchain ID can track his or her performance during the entire working life. His or her performance is a constant with a blockchain ID given that goes wherever he or she goes. An intern with a Creamchain ID creates permanent performance ratings for over four or five decades, which can be compared with any other Creamchain ID globally. The significant aspect of Creamchain ID is the energy force it represents, without gender bias. To become an independent director or a CEO this would be useful, as the records are of performance in both the fields - fiscal assets and ethical assets. The question of how many women are a part of the board of directors is passé.

Ashoka's edicts, for example, 9 (Protection of all religions) and 11 (Well-learned in the good doctrines of other people's religions) are going to be critical for global harmony. As part of GNH and identifying individuals could be the answer to these chaotic times. Modern civilizational progress rests on accountability and ownership, which Creamchain as a concept of combined personal performance with a personal ID ensures sustainability of efficiency and sustainability of value creation.

Audit Profession

The audit profession is one of the most highly respected professions in the world. Society does not influence a company, but adds mass to it, because of the audit profession. It is the only profession entrusted with certifying corporate affairs as a trustee of society. GRACE - governance, responsibility, authority, credibility, enabled fiscal assets, and ethical assets - is the hallmark of adding mass to the respective organizations. Society does not add mass directly but through its trustee, the audit profession.

The Institute of Chartered Accountants of India (ICAI) was formed by an Act of Parliament in 1949. It is said Sri Aurobindo[9] selected a passage from the *Kathopanishad*[10] as its motto, in its logo that exists today. The motto of ICAI is "ya Esha supteshu jagarti" in Sanskrit, meaning "who, this, while we are asleep, remains awake." This passage, Swami Chinmayananda[11] explains with the analogy of a streetlight. The light illuminates everything it comes across - a honeymooning couple enjoying their time, a drunkard reveling in stupor, or a mournful procession of a sad funeral pyre that passes by - but the streetlight itself remains untouched by any of the emotions. This verily is That. Self is not an object of senses and in all the three states of consciousness - waking state, dream state, and deep sleep state - it remains unperturbed. The audit profession is an unbiased observer of corporate affairs. Selecting this passage from the *Upanishad*, Sri Aurobindo, who influenced brilliant minds world over from Sri Aurobindo Ashram, suggested the role a chartered accountant (CA) should follow. Not to be disturbed by what is revealed within corporate but to focus on the duty that the audit profession has entrusted to a CA.

Being an observer and remaining unperturbed is not being indifferent. The audit profession has taken it literally, declaring, "The auditor is a watchdog, not a bloodhound." With cases such as HP - Autonomy, Carillion, and IL&FS offering a major setback to the profession, its credibility and ability to ferret out fraud and misdeeds are in question. Society needs the audit profession, entrusted with the explication of laws and management quality. These laws are designed as a cat's claws and teeth, benevolent to the kitten but malevolent to the rat.

The audit profession is not the sole caretaker of society. A CA is a CA wherever he or she is. A CA in a company should be given statutory powers as much as a statutory auditor gets. A CFO when entrusted with such powers, similar to the statutory auditor, can deal with the kitten and with the rat internally as deemed fit. A CFO is indeed a trustee of society. To quote Peter Drucker: The first organization structure of the modern West was laid down in the canon law of the Catholic Church eight hundred years ago. It set up a strictly scalar organization. But most of the provisions in the canon law that deal with the structure and organization of the Catholic Church define those things which only the parish priest, i.e., the bottom man in the pyramid, can do in his parish. The bishop appoints him; and, within clear procedural limits, the bishop can remove him.[12] Similarly, the law must be enacted such that a CFO can be removed only in an EGM of shareholders.

During the Lockheed, Gulf Oil scandal, Walter E. Hanson, the CEO of Peat Marwick, moved to restore confidence by volunteering to have his company's procedures audited by colleagues from competing firms. Today, the Big 8 firms have shrunk to the Big 4 firms, as no one knows who the partners are or which firm they belong to unless brought to notice by law agencies, as happened in the PwC audit fiasco of Satyam computers. Audit firms must follow the same Corporate Atomic Structure, Return on Intangible principle, with Index of Inactivity by Resource Area and Process Area for all their activities: (1) Audit & Assurance (2) Tax, (3) Advisory, and (4) Business Services. Quality targets set and performed must also apply to them, from foot soldier to senior partner. Change the denominator.

Corporate Citizenship

Recently there was a request from the chairman of GIDC, with ethical responsibility as the prime motive, regarding whether our team could implement a digital solution to clear out the never-ending corruption hounding the organization. Spread over the whole of Gujarat, executing several land deals, corruption within it seems inevitable. With the introduction of the CREAM Report, it is possible to bring in a digital solution. But I told my team, in 2020 we are celebrating the 150th Birth Anniversary of Mahatma Gandhi; it would be better the chief minister declares Gujarat a corruption-free government. Identifying one organization for the anti-corruption drive is not recommended while there are so many others that are equally afflicted by corruption. But Gujarat is in an outstanding position for an anti-corruption drive, not only because Mahatma Gandhi was born there but also due to the introduction of prohibition in the state since formation on May 1, 1960. The social benefits of prohibition should be compared with the situation of another state, Tamil Nadu, where there is no prohibition. Tamil Nadu government revenue is dependent on the sale of liquor through the Tamil Nadu State Marketing Corporation (TASMAC) liquor shops. In Tamil Nadu particularly womenfolk suffer a lot and they do favor voting for a party that could introduce prohibition. Alas, there is no such party contesting with prohibition in their election manifesto. For Gujarat, it is a remarkable journey of social benefits.

The social aspects of the management of national agenda rest with the governments. In India, CSR expenditure is mandatory for companies with certain given criteria. The ethical motive for corporate is embedded for corporate at the time of company registration itself. For example, UNCAC is mandatory for corporate in countries where UNCAC is ratified. India is one such country. However, UNCAC is in limbo because of Article 6, Preventive anti-corruption body or bodies are not invoked. Once ratified UNCAC is mandatory, particularly for corporate under Article 12, Private Sector, whether an anti-corruption body is created or not, for companies while dealing with another country where UNCAC stands ratified. Two countries, Barbados and Syria, have not ratified UNCAC out of 187 states parties.

"Corporate citizenship involves the social responsibility of businesses and the extent to which they meet legal, ethical, and economic responsibilities, as established by shareholders. Corporate citizenship is growing increasingly important as both individual and institutional investors begin to seek out companies that have socially responsible orientations such as their environmental, social, and governance (ESG) practices."[13] This book is a systematic appraisal of CSR, split into Corporate Fiscal Responsibility and Corporate Ethical Responsibility. It goes further with the CREAM Report covering the provisions of all published standards, such as ISO 26000 Social Responsibility, by way of an add-on process block under management quality. This would come under the four auxiliary limbs of the corporate body, explication of corporate laws and management quality. Once a company adopts the published standards, such as ISO 26000 Social Responsibility, the activation process takes place for the implementation of such standards. This is done through people's energy, calculated by Return on

Intangible, by Subject - Object Distinction of Qualitative and Quantitative Elements of Management. The action process justifies adherence to standards. Corporate gets the ratings, accordingly, on the basis of the ratings obtained from individuals exerting their energy.

Society, as the corporate neutron, does not influence the corporate identity but adds mass to it. While doing so society adds mass to the nucleus with its partner, the corporate proton - the board of directors and shareholders. It stabilizes the running of the corporate electron spinning around the said nucleus, for a Goldilocks effect. Society, therefore, enables corporate citizenship in the right direction. When the six main limbs and four auxiliary limbs are working together shipshape, as illustrated in Chapter 6, one can see corporate in human form. A company seen now as an entity is bereft of that pulsating energy. Citizenship is always for individuals, not for an entity. To qualify for a Corporate citizenship, the men and women in each organization alone are entitled for it. It is therefore in order that the Creamchain contains individuals in the list of corporate citizenship, with the company they work for in a secondary list. Corporate citizenship is constant, the corresponding company is not.

Chapter 9: Points to Ponder

1. Knowledge is the goal of ethics: Society provides stability to the Corporate/Government Atomic Structure lest the electrons spin too fast to go off tangent. Transparency justifies companies' conduct, which is the societal good. The goal of ethical motive is the knowledge of societal good. Accumulation and retention of such knowledge is the goal of ethics.
2. Just and equitable Society, the 11 challenges: "Amidst the tens of thousands of names of monarchs that crowd the columns of history ... the name of Ashoka shines and shines almost alone a star."
3. Creamchain: Foundation for Happiness Index
    I Happiness Index
    1. The 2019 *Global Happiness and Wellbeing Policy Report*. The 2019 *World Happiness Report* 2019: The report is produced by the United Nations Sustainable Development Solutions Network.

II Ranking of Happiness Report
2. The 2019 *World Happiness Report*
III GDP
3. "Happiness: Towards a Holistic Approach to Development," Draft note: 1. WEIRD and 2 - (i) recognize that GDP is not the only indicator of well-being, - (ii) integrate economic and social policies better, (iii) develop specific policies for environmental protection, (iv) develop well-being indicators to guide their policy design and monitoring in line with sustainable development objectives.
IV GNH
4. "Gross National Happiness vs Gross Domestic Product": In Bhutan, "Gross National Happiness is more important than Gross National Product." GDP data needs to be thoroughly overhauled.
V. Integrate GDP and GNH. Blueprint GSDP of $1.5 trillion, 2024, Strategy Plan.

EPP - efforts per person

Both GDP and GNH go together not one versus the other.

4. Creamchain: Modern civilizational progress rests on accountability and ownership, which Creamchain as a concept of combined personal performance with a personal ID ensures.
5. Audit profession: It is the only profession entrusted with the responsibility to certify corporate affairs as a trustee of the society. GRACE - governance, responsibility, authority, credibility, enabled fiscal assets, and ethical assets - is the hallmark of adding mass to the respective organizations.
6. The motto of ICAI is "ya Esha supteshu jagarti" in Sanskrit, meaning "who, this, while we are asleep, remains awake." It is a tribute to audit and accounting professionals, who are vigilant always.
7. Society needs the audit profession, entrusted with the explication of laws and management quality, as these laws are designed as a cat's claws and teeth, benevolent to the kitten but malevolent to the rat.

8. Audit firms must follow the same Corporate Atomic Structure principle.
9. Corporate Citizenship: Citizenship is always for individuals. Corporate citizenship personifies the people behind who have been bestowed with it, as listed in Creamchain.

Action Points

1. A CFO is entrusted with such powers, similar to the statutory auditor, as to deal internally with the kitten and the rat as deemed fit.

Notes

1. The Edicts of Ashoka: https://www.cs.colostate.edu/~malaiya/ashoka.html.
2. Global Happiness and Wellbeing Policy Report 2019, management by Sharon Paculor, copy edit by Rebecca Clapperton Law and Sybil Fares. ISBN 978-0-9968513-8-1.
3. World Happiness Report management by Sharon Paculor, copy edit by Sweta Gupta, Sybil Fares and Ismini Ethridge.: ISBN 978-0-9968513-9-8.
4. Luis.Collantes https://www.un.org/esa/socdev/ageing/documents/NOTEONHAPPINESSFINALCLEAN.pdf
5. Ms. Yeshu (International Research Journal of Commerce Arts and Science http://www.casirj.com https://www.academia.edu/27198395/Gross_National_Happiness_Vs_Gross_Domestic_Product?auto=download).
6. Luis Collantes: https://www.un.org/esa/socdev/ageing/documents/NOTEONHAPPINESSFINALCLEAN.pdf.
7. Economic Survey 2019–2020 Statistical Appendix: 1.10 A Net State Domestic Product at Current Prices (2011–2012 Series).
8. Blockchain Technology Overview: https://doi.org/10.6028/NIST.IR.8202.
9. Sri Aurobindo. https://www.sriaurobindoashram.org/sriaurobindo/.
10. Kathopanishad (Chapter II, Valli v, Mantra #8).
11. Swami Chinmayananda. http://www.chinmayamission.com/who-we-are/swami-chinmayananda/.
12. Management Tasks and responsibilities: Peter F. Drucker: TRUMAN TALLEY BOOKS / E.P. DUTTON / New York.
13. Investopedia: https://www.investopedia.com/terms/c/corporatecitizenship.asp.

About the Author

Jayaraman Rajah Iyer, Chartered Accountant (ICAI, New Delhi, 1966), has a unique insight into major changes in accounting, culled from experience with firms across the globe. He interned at Hindustan Lever (1966) and held key positions at Automobile Products of India (API) and Mafatlal Services. As Forestry Operations Accountant at Wimco (1972), he introduced "Likely Ultimate Cost." In 1977 he was General Manager of ITI, Lagos, Nigeria. Sir William Castell, who later became Chairman of the Wellcome Trust, selected him to join the Wellcome Foundation, UK, specifically to set right the dysfunctional accounting at Wellcome, Nigeria. During the 1990s he was engaged in corporate consulting. He had been visiting faculty at SIES School of Management, where he taught balanced scorecard and strategic cost management on the basis of the Proprietary IBCM (inactivity based cost management, 2006, copyright © Jayaraman Iyer). He has been a crusader against corruption and business malpractice all through his life. His mission is to convert corporate to adopt return on intangible for accelerating growth and profits. He believes the utilization of men and women employed as of now amounts to nothing, knowing their amazing capabilities that are immense. Intangible is a powerhouse that when triggered would bring prosperity and happiness to all around. Value System is crucial to bring the abstractions into reality, acknowledge value where value is due, and deconstruct what is valueless. A Sustainable Value System within corporate would bring in sustainable profits, he avers. A well-managed corporate will have no chance of getting muddled with NPAs and interest defaults. For this return on intangible is the only solution, he emphasizes. His call for Change, Change, Change Corporate, Change the Denominator is to usher in people's energy as the basis for measuring development and well-being. India's culture should be carried forward, forever, as it is intangible, he says.

Index

Aadhar Card, 102
Action Process, 27–28, 59–62, 68–69, 76–77
   properties of, 77–78
   ratings for, 77
Action Value Capital, 78
American Online (AOL), 45
Apple, 70
Arthapatti, 112
Artificial intelligence, 101–102
Ashland Oil Inc., 81
Ashoka's edicts, 123–124, 131
Atomic structure
   benchmarking corporate atomic structure aligning with, 89
   similarity between corporate atomic structure and, 86
Audit profession, 132–133
Authority, 44, 51

Barings Bank, 82
Bayer, 2
Big Bang, 27
Blockchain technology, 131
Board of Banking Supervision, 82
Board of directors, 102–105
Brahma Sutra, 32

Capitalism, definition of, 20
Capital–Output Ratio, 113–114
Carillion, 2, 3
Causality, 1–15
Chartered accountant (CA), 132–133
Code of business principles (CoBP), 6, 7, 75
Code of Conduct (CoC). *See* Code of business principles (CoBP)
Committee of Sponsoring Organizations of the Treadway Commission (COSO) Framework, 23, 24, 55, 75

Control Environment, definition of, 23
Corporate atomic structure, 84–89, 95
   007 factor, 88–89
   benchmarking, aligning with atomic structure, 89
   similarity between atomic structure and, 86
Corporate body
   four auxiliary limbs of, 97
   six limbs of, 96
Corporate citizenship, 133–135
Corporate Critical Density, 99–100
   artificial intelligence, 101–102
   board of directors, 102–105
   reverse mentoring, 105–106
   sustainability, 100
Corporate electron, CREAM Report for, 109–119
Corporate ethical responsibility (CER), 4–5
Corporate Ethics, 93
Corporate fiscal responsibility (CFR), 4
Corporate governance, 9, 112
Corporate neutron. *See* Society, for corporate neutron
Corporate proton, 99–106
Corporate social responsibility (CSR), 4
Corporate structure, 62
Corporate Yoga, 94
COVID-19, 91, 106
CREAM analytics framework, 91–92
CREAM Report
   for corporate electron, 109–119
   deeper commitment with, 114–115
   Hindustan Unilever Limited, 110–112

142   INDEX

CREAM Report (*continued*)
   rating, 105
   spot your place, 115–116
Creamchain, 130–132
Creative Process, 27, 56, 59, 60–62, 68, 91
   properties of, 77–78
   ratings for, 74
Credibility, 44, 51–52

3-D Corporate Atomic Structure, 85–86
Data explosion, 95

Economic disasters, 22–23
Effort transforms mass into energy, 59–60
Efforts per person (EPP), 127–130
Emergent property phenomenon, 94–97
Enabled balance sheet, 44, 52
Enterprise resource planning (ERP), 101
Ethical assets, 9, 35, 88–89, 99, 130
Ethical Assets Premium Account, 116
Ethical Responsibility (ER), 93, 105, 121–123, 133, 134
Ethical Strategy Plan, 75
European Organization for Nuclear Research (CERN), 11–13, 67
   Shiva's cosmic dance statue, 12
Exchange rate crisis, 45

Farmer producer companies (FPCs), 102, 114
Farmer producer organisations (FPOs), 102, 114
Federation of Industries and Associations (FIA), 127
Fiduciary responsibility, 1
Financial Crisis Advisory Group (FCAG), 49
Food and Drug Administration (FDA), 6
Food and Drug Administration (FDA) Modernization Act (1997), 25–26
Foreign Corrupt Practices Act (FCPA), 22, 42

G-R-A-C-E, 44–51, 132
G-R-A-C-E Version 2, 51–52
General Motors, 70
GenNext, 106
Global Happiness Index, 124
"Goldilocks Effect," 100
Good manufacturing practice (GMP), 6
Governance, 44, 51, 83
Government Auditing Standards, 83
Gross domestic product (GDP), 126–127
Gross National Happiness (GNH) Index, 126–127
Gujarat state domestic product (GSDP), 127–130

Happiness Index, 124–125
Hedonism, 21–22
Hewlett-Packard (HP), 2
Hindustan Unilever Limited CREAM Report, 110–112

IAS 9, 1977, 42–43
IAS 38, 41, 46
Implication, 63–64
Inactivity Based Cost Management (IBCM), 81–97
   corporate atomic structure, 84–89
   emergent property phenomenon, 94–97
   governance gets measured and managed, 81–83
   measure qualitative elements, 84
   return on intangible, 90–94
Index of inactivity (IA)
   by process area, 103, 110–112
   by resource area, 104, 110–112
Indian Brand Equity Foundation (IBEF) report, 102
Indian Companies Act 2013, 23–26
India's GDP, 115–116
Industrial Credit and Investment Corporation of India (ICICI), 3
Industrial Development Bank of India (IDBI), 3
Infosys, 2

Infrastructure Leasing & Financial Services (IL&FS), 2, 28, 37
Innovation, 27, 56, 62, 91
Insolvency and Bankruptcy Code (IBC), 9
Instinctive, 10
Institute of Chartered Accountants of India (ICAI), 132
Intangible
  defined, 61–62
  implication, 63–64
  search for, 56
  opposite values, 56–58
Intangible assets, 41–53
  definition of, 41, 46
  G-R-A-C-E, 44–51
  G-R-A-C-E Version 2, 51–52
  IAS 9, 1977, 42–43
Intangible, measuring, 67–80
  Action Process, 68–69, 76–77
  Action Value Capital, 78
  corporate transformation cause, 69–75
  creation of substance, 67–68
  Creative Process, 68
  Intangible Value Capital, 78–79
  Intellectual Value Capital, 75–76
Intangible Value Capital, 78–79
Intellectual property (IP), 48, 49
Intellectual property right (IPR), 27, 49
Intellectual Value Capital, 75–76
International Accounting Standards Board (IASB), 41
International Accounting Standards Committee (IASC), 41, 43, 44, 46
International Covenant on Economic, Social and Cultural Rights (1966), 7
International Finance Corporation (IFC), 3
ISO 26000 Social Responsibility, 134–135

Keynes's Animal Spirits, 24–25, 73
"Know Thyself," 32–33
Knowledge is goal of ethics, 25–26
KPMG–EIU survey, 84

Lamborghini, 3
Large Hadron Collider (LHC), 27
Lehman Brothers, 83
Linga, 112
Lockheed Aircraft Corp., 22
London Inter-bank Offered Rate (LIBOR), 13

MAGA (Make America Great Again) campaign, 19–20
Micro, small and medium enterprises (MSME), 3, 61
Micron Technology, 45
Microsoft, 42, 45, 70
Monsanto, 2
Morality, 21
Motorola, 45
Mutual funds, 48

National Aeronautics and Space Administration (NASA), 30, 42, 67, 70–71
National Institute of Standards and Technology (NIST), 131
Newton's First Law of Motion, 27–28, 89
Newton's Second Law of Motion, 90
Non-performing assets (NPAs), 3, 9, 72, 99

Opposite Value Analysis, 95
Opposite values, 56–57
  study of, 57–58

Organisation for Economic Co-operation and Development (OECD), 22, 51, 62, 95, 131
Organizational restructuring, 84

Plato's Cave, 12–14
  corporate is living in, 14
Process Blocks, 92–93
Project FISCAL (farmer–industry–society & consolidate agri leadership), 102
Pulsating energy, 26–35

144 INDEX

Reliance Industries, 70
Reserve Bank of Australia, 82
Responsibility, 44, 51
Return on intangible, 90–94
Reverse mentoring, 105–106

Sage of Kanchi, 58
Sankalpa, 115–116
SAP Software Solutions, 35
Sarbanes–Oxley Act (SOX), 22, 55
Self-governance, 33, 72–73, 93, 121
Serious Fraud Investigation Office (SFIO), 14
Societal good, 3, 4, 8, 122
Society, for corporate neutron, 121–137
  audit profession, 131–133
  corporate citizenship, 133–135
  creamchain, 130–132
Spreadsheet Organization Structure, 62
State morality. *See* Ashoka's edicts
Strategy Plan, 69, 77
  deeper commitment with CREAM Report, 114–115
Subject - Object Distinction of Qualitative and Quantitative Elements of Management, 135
Substance
  creation of, 67–68
  transformation stages, 69–75
Substance of Quality, 68, 73–74
Sustainability, 30, 84, 100
  of efficiency, 88, 97, 115
  of profits, 35, 88, 97, 115
  of value system, 88, 97, 115
Sustainable Living Plan project, 4

Tamil Nadu State Marketing Corporation (TASMAC), 134
Tata Group, 2

Tesla, 70
Toshiba, 2
Total quality management (TQM), 6
Transparency, 122
Truth, 56

UN World Economic Survey report 1977, 43
UNCAC Article 10, Public Reporting, 5, 26, 122
UNCAC Article 12, Private Sector, 134
UNCAC Article 13, Participation of Society, 5, 25, 122
UNCAC Article 46, Mutual Legal Assistance, 76
Unilever, 4, 70
United Nations Convention Against Corruption (UNCAC), 5, 68, 75–76, 134
United Nations Global Compact (UNGC), 6, 68
United Nations Millennium Declaration, 3
U.S. Government Accountability Office, 83
U.S. Securities and Exchange Commission (SEC), 46

Volkswagen, 2, 7, 23–24

What you see is what you get (WYSIWYG), 32
Whistleblower Policy, 6, 76, 111, 112
World Commission on Environment and Development, 100
World Economic and Social Survey 1995, 47
World Happiness Report, 125–126

007 factor, 88–89

OTHER TITLES IN OUR BUSINESS ETHICS AND CORPORATE CITIZENSHIP COLLECTION

David Wasieleski, Duquesne University, *Editor*

- *Powerful Performance: How to Be Influential, Ethical, and Successful in Business* by Mark Eyre
- *Applied Humanism: How to Create More Effective and Ethical Businesses* by Jennifer Hancock

BEP is also proud to have books in our Giving Voice to Values on Business Ethics and Corporate Social Responsibility Collection, including these

- *Educating Business Professionals: The Call Beyond Competence and Expertise* by Lana S. Nino
- *Adapting to Change: The Business of Climate Resilience* by Ann Goodman
- *Social Media Ethics Made Easy: How to Comply with FTC Guidelines* by Joseph W. Barnes
- *Sales Ethics: How To Sell Effectively While Doing the Right Thing* by Alberto Aleo
- *Engaging Millennials for Ethical Leadership: What Works For Young Professionals and Their Managers* by Jessica McManus Warnell
- *War Stories: Fighting, Competing, Imagining, Leading* by Leigh Hafrey
- *Working Ethically in Finance: Clarifying Our Vocation* by Anthony Asher
- *Shaping the Future of Work: What Future Worker, Business, Government, and Education Leaders Need To* by Thomas A. Kochan
- *The ART of Responsible Communication: Leading with Values Every Day* by David L. Remund
- *Ethical Leadership in Sport: What's Your ENDgame* by Pippa Grange

Announcing the Business Expert Press Digital Library

Concise e-books business students need for classroom and research

This book can also be purchased in an e-book collection by your library as

- a one-time purchase,
- that is owned forever,
- allows for simultaneous readers,
- has no restrictions on printing, and
- can be downloaded as PDFs from within the library community.

Our digital library collections are a great solution to beat the rising cost of textbooks. E-books can be loaded into their course management systems or onto students' e-book readers.

The **Business Expert Press** digital libraries are very affordable, with no obligation to buy in future years. For more information, please visit **www.businessexpertpress.com/librarians**. To set up a trial in the United States, please email **sales@businessexpertpress.com**.

www.ingramcontent.com/pod-product-compliance
Lightning Source LLC
Chambersburg PA
CBHW052101230426
43662CB00036B/1720